W9-AFR-783

Contributions
of Women

ART

by Carol Fowler

DISTRIBUTED BY

NATIONAL WOMEN'S HISTORY PROJECT
Box 3716   Santa Rosa, CA 95402 (707) 526-5974

Dillon Press, Inc.
Minneapolis, Minnesota

Library of Congress Cataloging in Publication Data

Fowler, Carol.
   Art.

   (Contributions of women)
   Bibliography: p. 150
   SUMMARY: Brief biographies of six prominent American
women artists: Mary Cassatt, Grandma Moses, Georgia
O'Keeffe, Louise Nevelson, Helen Frankenthaler, and Su-
zanne Jackson.
   1. Women artists — United States — Biography — Juvenile
literature. [1. Women artists—United States. 2. Artists] I.
Title.
N6536.F64   709'.2'2[B] [920]   76-3479
ISBN 0-87518-115-5

Dillon Press, Inc., 500 South Third Street
Minneapolis, Minnesota 55415

Printed in the United States of America

Contents

The photographs are reproduced through the courtesy of the Ankrum Gallery, Los Angeles; The Art Institute of Chicago; André Emmerich Gallery, New York; Galerie St. Etienne, New York; Lynn Gilbert; Grandma Moses Properties, Inc., New York; Juan Hamilton; Wayne Leonard; Al Mozell; The Museum of Modern Art, New York; The National Gallery of Art, Washington, D.C.; The Pace Gallery, New York; and Edward Youkilis.

Introduction

Although young women have always been encouraged to draw and to paint, becoming a professional painter or sculptor has never been easy, either for a man or a woman. But there have always been serious artists, who happen to have been women also. This book presents the life stories of six of them.

Each of the artists presented has made, or is making, outstanding contributions to her special area of art. Each has won the highest awards and honors of the art world. Some of them have been the first women to receive certain awards, paving the way for those who follow. As it hangs in museums side by side with the work of male artists, there is no way to distinguish the work of the women, except as the work of one artist is different from that of another.

The subjects these artists chose to portray vary from simple farm scenes to the most modern, abstract painting. The materials they have used range from delicate pastels to heavy welded metals for modern sculpture. Their styles reflect all periods of art. In fact, reading their lives in chronological order is a lesson in modern art history.

None of the six women has been a feminist; their paintings and sculptures alone speak for the unlimited horizons of women's talent. Their journey toward this horizon may chart a route for us to follow.

Mary Cassatt, an American artist, played an important part in the French impressionist movement.

A Career in Paris

MARY CASSATT

By the time Mary Cassatt turned sixteen in the spring of 1860, she already knew that she wanted to be an artist. A great artist. Pretty watercolors of flowers and trees did not interest her. She wanted to paint fine oil portraits.

Many times Mary had tried to sketch the children who played in Penn Square across the street from the Cassatt family home in Philadelphia. Sometimes she was able to make pencil drawings that looked just like them. But at other times, if an arm lay at an awkward angle or if a face was too deep in shadow, she could not draw what she saw—no matter how hard she tried. She realized she needed training to be an artist.

Mary remembered her parents talking about the fine art museums and the wonderful schools in countries like Italy, France and Germany. She remembered, too, her older brother, Alexander, had studied science and engineering in Europe for five years, and the entire Cassatt family had lived there with him. If only she could go to Rome to study art!

She dreaded talking to her father about studying abroad. But Mary's nature was honest and direct, and one day she simply brought up the subject and asked his permission. Mr. Cassatt was shocked. The idea of being a professional artist was unusual for a man, and unthinkable for a woman. Perhaps watercolor lessons at home would be appropriate for Mary. Young ladies in Philadelphia at that time were expected to know how to use watercolors and how to embroider.

But Mary stood firm. To her, art was not a hobby to dabble at in her spare time. She wanted to learn how to paint well in a real studio and have the best training possible.

When Mr. Cassatt saw how serious Mary was, he considered taking the family to Rome. Alexander, who had now finished school, offered to stay in the United States and take over his father's brokerage and banking interests. But then in 1861 the Civil War began, and it was not possible for anyone to go to Europe.

Mary decided instead to enroll in the Pennsylvania Academy of Fine Arts, the oldest art school in the country. For the Cassatts, a proud, prominent Philadelphia family, the idea of their daughter attending a professional school to study for a career was strange indeed. But they accepted their daughter's wishes.

In the fall of 1861, Mary entered the Pennsylvania Academy and began drawing in what was called an "antiques class." Perched on stools, the class drew pencil sketches of statues from the academy's collection. Actually, the statues were plaster copies of ancient Greek and Roman marble statues. Mary very quickly mastered the technique of copying the statues.

Besides the antiques class, Mary also attended anatomy classes at Penn Medical University. Seeing human dissections helped her understand how the body is shaped by the bones and muscles underneath. Occasionally she went to see paintings and statues in private homes in Philadelphia. But at that time Americans did not own many art works, and the quality was ordinary.

After a year of copying statues at the academy, Mary grew impatient. White plaster did not offer the challenge of real skin tones. And the profile and body proportions of the statues were always perfect. Mary admitted that her own chin might be a bit too pointed or that she might be too tall and thin, but that was the way she looked. Real people were not perfect.

In the academy's "life class," students drew from live models. But the Pennsylvania Academy had a rule that women could not take the life class. They thought that women would be embarrassed by being in the same class with men, because the models posed in the nude. Mary and another student, Eliza Haldeman, thought the rule was silly, and Eliza organized a life class for women students. Mary and Eliza took turns posing for each other.

After two years in drawing classes, academy students were finally allowed to paint with oils. Mary applied for permission to copy a portion of *Deliverance of Leyden,* a very large oil painting. She soon found that copying was a fine way to understand how the original artist had solved problems of color, space, and balance. This method of copying masterpieces was important to Mary's training as an artist. She continued to use it, and years later she often advised young art students to do the same.

Mary learned all she could in her four years at the Pennsylvania Academy, but when she was finished she still felt like a student. Since the Civil War was now over, Mary approached her father again about study in Europe. At last Mr. Cassatt arranged for her to live with family friends in Paris.

After her arrival in Paris, Mary enrolled in the studio of Charles Chaplin. Chaplin, like other established painters, usually allowed a few art students to set up their easels and work in his studio. In this way, students could see a professional artist at work. In turn, the artist would give them advice on their own paintings.

Following the style popular at that time, Charles Chaplin draped deep folds of cloth around his models from the waist down. He told Mary to paint the skin in very rosy tones and to make the cloth look like a heavy, expensive fabric. Sometimes Mary thought the model looked pale and thin, not rosy at all. Instead of the luxurious drapes, she would choose a more simple garment. Charles Chaplin warned Mary that if she did not paint in the popular style, her work would never be chosen to hang in the Salon.

The Salon was the name the French gave to an art exhibit held every year in Paris. Mary had attended the first Salon exhibit during her childhood, when the Cassatts were in Paris for Alexander's schooling. She still remembered that the paintings hung over the entire walls from the floor to the ceiling. Paintings accepted for the Salon were chosen by a jury from the French Academy of Painters and Sculptors. They chose only those things that they considered to be in the "proper" style.

It was important for artists to have their paintings exhibited at the Salon. Artists who won prizes there became famous, and paintings accepted at the Salon sometimes sold for large sums of money. But Mary felt uncomfortable about trying to paint everything in rich, rosy tones as Charles Chaplin insisted. It was as unnatural as the white statues at the Pennsylvania Academy. Finally, after a short time, she decided to leave his studio.

In the summer of 1869 Mary traveled to the mountains in southeastern France on a sketching tour. She loved sketching the healthy-looking farmers, and their costumes were more interesting than the draped fabrics of the studio models.

After she returned to Paris, Mary received a letter from her father. He knew that France and Germany were having political troubles, and he insisted that Mary return to Philadelphia. Mary hated to interrupt her work, but it was lucky that she left. Shortly afterward the Franco-Prussian War began, and eventually the Germans surrounded Paris completely. Food was scarce, and the only contact between the city and the rest of France was by balloon.

In Philadelphia, Mary continued to paint and learn. Even now, she was not always successful. Her brother, Alexander, had married by then and had a young son named Eddie. Mary painted an overly ambitious, full-length portrait of Eddie, standing stiffly before a pleated curtain. She was far more skilled at painting people in natural poses.

Later Mary traveled to Chicago and took along several small paintings, hoping to sell them in the Midwest. One evening in Chicago they noticed the red glow of a fire. At first they ignored it, but the fire, driven by winds, raced through the city. They hurried to their hotel, picked up their bags, and ran. This was the Great Chicago Fire of 1871. Unfortunately, all of Mary's paintings were burned in this fire.

Upset by the loss, Mary returned to Europe. She went to Parma, Italy, where she studied paintings by the Italian master Correggio. Most of Correggio's works were painted directly on the walls of the cathedral. Each day she carried a sketch pad or easel and paints and copied the babies and mothers. She loved the healthy-looking, sturdy babies. She studied intently the tones and colors of the skin to understand how Correggio could have created such real-looking infants. Many years later, Mary told her French biographer, Achille Segard, "For eight months I went to school to Correggio." And her interest in painting mothers and children continued throughout her life.

Next she traveled to Madrid, where she studied Spanish masters at the Prado Museum. Besides copying old masterpieces, Mary worked on her own oil paintings. They were done in a style that reflected the Spanish paintings she studied at the Prado. Bright, highlighted areas are contrasted to deeply shadowed areas. She sent a balcony scene of three people at the Carnival in Seville to the Paris Salon of 1872. Since she did not have the nerve to submit it under her full name, she used her middle name with her first name—Mary Stevenson. To her great delight, the Salon accepted her painting. In 1873 her painting of a bullfighter and a young girl, done with broad brush strokes, was accepted. This time she signed it Mary S. Cassatt.

In the Prado Museum, she also discovered the paintings of the Flemish master Peter Paul Rubens. She was so excited by the vigor and rich colors of his paintings that she hurried to Antwerp, Belgium, to study more of his work.

After two years of copying old European masters, Mary felt it was time for her to develop her own style. Where could she settle? She still needed the stimulation of fine paintings and contact with other artists—things found in Europe. Yet, the Cassatts were a close family, and she missed her parents and the rest of the family in the United States. When her mother visited her in Antwerp in 1873, Mary must have discussed this hard decision.

In the end, she chose Paris, which at that time was the art center of the world. This turned out to be an important decision, because she spent most of her life, from then on, in France. In the next few years Mary painted on her own and also continued her study of old masterpieces at the Louvre, one of the finest museums in the world.

Mary's skills increased. The Salon of 1874 accepted her *Madame Cortier,* a portrait of a middle-aged woman with bright red hair. When Edgar Degas, an artist who later became very important to Mary, saw it, he paused to examine the plump face, wavy hair, and pleasant smile of the subject. He recognized that the artist could draw skillfully and had prepared for the portrait carefully. Degas commented to a friend that this artist felt as he did—that her work was "true." Mary had submitted the painting under the name Mary Cassatt, and she signed her work in this way for the rest of her life.

Though three years would pass before they actually met each other, Mary had already discovered Degas' work in a similar way. In a shop window on the Boulevard Haussmann, she peered at a pastel drawing of ballet dancers at rehearsal. One ballerina frowned and rubbed her arched back. Another practiced a difficult position. The footlights of the theatre seemed to shine through their gauze skirts, drawn with pale strokes of the chalk. Mary read the signature—Degas.

When she told other artists about discovering the work by Degas, they told her a little more about him. He was very brilliant, but his personality was difficult. He could be quarrelsome, and he always said exactly what he thought.

Degas belonged to a group of artists called the "impressionists," who had rebelled against the rigid rules of the Salon. They held their own exhibitions, and they did not have a jury to choose certain paintings; all of the paintings were exhibited. Their name came from a painting called *Impression,* a colorful sunrise which had been shown in their first exhibit. Newspaper articles of the time ridiculed the paintings—these were mere impressions, not art works at all. The public, too, openly laughed at the bright paintings that lacked the careful, formal qualities of Salon paintings. Today, however, impressionists' paintings are highly prized by collectors of art. This was the movement that started modern art.

The impressionists painted light reflected from objects or people in bright, fresh colors. Water shimmering in the sun was painted in short, curved strokes of blue, gray, and white paint. The leaves of a tree were daubs not only of green, but of blue, yellow, or white. This was a new way of seeing things, an artist's new vision.

The vivid colors used by the impressionists appealed to Mary, and she began to make some of her own works brighter. She also began painting things on a light background, as the impressionists did. The background for the portrait she submitted to the Salon of 1875 was pale, rather than the traditional dark background. The jury rejected the painting. She decided to test the jury, and repainted the background in what she called the "brown sauce of the Salon." In 1876 it hung in the Salon. After that, Mary never bothered to send the Salon anything more.

One day in 1877, a man with a dark beard and heavy eyelids knocked at Mary's door. It was Degas. Nervously Mary glanced behind her, trying to remember which paintings were out. He would see them, and she had heard about his severe opinions. But before he noticed anything, he invited Mary to join the impressionists. Mary accepted without hesitating an instant. She liked their new, colorful style of painting and agreed with their practice of accepting everything for their exhibitions.

Degas continued to visit Mary's studio often. Sometimes he paged through a set of drawings, complimenting those he thought were well done. He dismissed others with a grunt. She respected his opinions and ideas about the need to draw and compose a painting well.

In 1877 her parents and her sister Lydia came to live permanently in Paris. Mary rented an apartment on the sixth floor of a building on the Avenue Trudaine, just at the base of Monmartre, the hill where Degas and many other artists lived. Mary's studio was nearby.

Mary enjoyed going to the new Paris Opéra with Lydia. Sometimes she sketched her sister sitting in the audience, and her portrait of Lydia at the Opéra hung in the fourth impressionist exhibit of 1879. Lydia's pink gown and orange-yellow hair glow in the reflected gaslight of the Opéra. A chandelier in the left background balances a row of balcony seats on the right. Mary captured the light of the impressionistic style and combined it with a strong balanced composition.

Lydia became Mary's favorite model. She painted her drinking tea, driving a horse and buggy, reading— and in the summer of 1880, crocheting in the garden at Marly, where the Cassatts had rented a villa for the summer. In the Marly painting, Lydia's healthy pink glow and smile of the Opéra portrait are lost. Her complexion appears pale. Gray shadows under her eyes hint at the Bright's disease from which she suffered.

Artistically, the painting was successful. In painting the fresh blue of Lydia's dress and the colorful garden, Mary used the color and light of impressionism in her own way. Degas said that the painting was more noble and firm than any work she had done before. Mary exhibited it at the sixth impressionist exhibition. A reviewer for a French newspaper wrote that she was no longer under anyone's influence. She now had a style of her own. She was pleased, but when her father pointed to the review, she answered, "Too much pudding," her favorite expression when she was embarrassed. She sold several paintings from this exhibition and used the money to buy paintings by Degas and other impressionists. She was building her own collection.

Growing daily weaker, Lydia posed for Mary only a few more times. She died of Bright's disease in November 1882. Mary missed her sister; not even in childhood had they been so close. For five years she had concentrated on Lydia's appearance and gestures as she tried to capture her in drawings and paintings. In the evenings they relaxed at the theater or with friends.

Then Alexander sent word that he was taking a leave from his successful job at the Pennsylvania Railroad to bring his family to Paris for a few months. The Cassatts looked forward to Christmas with the four young children. As on previous visits, the children would be lively subjects for Mary. More and more of her paintings now had children for their subjects. Mary had settled on the subject matter that would inspire her best work.

Mary made black and white prints from sketches of her nieces and nephews made during their visit. For her, printmaking was a new and ambitious technique, very different from oil painting. Degas had interested her in the idea of printmaking for a journal he wanted to publish. The process involves drawing lines with a hard needle on a copper plate. Thick, black printer's ink is rubbed into the lines. When the inked plate is run through a printing press with a sheet of paper, the ink sticks to the paper. In this way, a drawing can be reproduced many times over. Mary thought drawing on the plates was excellent practice. With no chance to erase or change the lines, her drawing had to be accurate and sure on the first try. Degas never published his journal, but the prints provided a fine record of this Christmas visit. And Mary had mastered another artistic medium.

By this time Degas had become an important influence in Mary's life and work. They never married, and it is not certain that they were in love. But they were very close friends. When Degas had argued with the impressionists over the arrangements for their seventh exhibition in 1882, he had withdrawn his paintings. In support, Mary had withdrawn also.

Sometimes she posed for him. But she did not always like the results. In one portrait he gave to her, she is seated and leans forward holding playing cards. She admired his skill in painting the difficult pose, but she disliked the image of herself. For a long time, she hung the portrait in her studio. But years later, when she asked her dealer, Durand-Ruel, to sell the painting, she asked him to list the subject as an unknown woman.

In late 1883 Mary noticed how difficult it was becoming for her mother to climb the six flights of stairs to the apartment. Mrs. Cassatt suffered from heart trouble. Mary decided to take her to Spain to recover in the warm climate. Mary loved the old walled city of

Alicante, but she hated to be away from her painting. Later they traveled to Biarritz, a city on the ocean. Mary left her mother there with a maid, Mathilde, and returned to Paris to rent a new, larger apartment with an elevator.

Her mother and father did not like the location of the new apartment and wanted to move. Getting them settled again was another distraction for Mary. Once in Paris, Durand-Ruel told her that he had sold two paintings and more were wanted. But she had not touched a brush for months.

When she finally was able to begin painting, her art entered a more mature period. The change was sparked by a quarrel with Degas. At the time, Mary was forty years old and beginning to be recognized in Paris as an accomplished artist. Yet Degas insisted that she still knew nothing about style. She was so angry that she refused to see him for weeks. She went to work on a painting that she hoped would prove he was wrong.

She chose to paint a side view of a girl seated in her nightgown. The pose she selected is an awkward one: The girl's left elbow is raised behind her head; her right hand holds a single braid of her hair in front of her body. A continuous line traced from her left arm, through her hair, and over her right arm would be a perfect curve, shaped like the letter S. The girl herself is not beautiful, her gown is very plain, and in the background is an ordinary washstand. Mary had deliberately made the success of the painting depend only on her own skill as an artist.

When Degas saw the painting at the eighth impressionist exhibition, he studied it for many minutes. Then he approached Mary. Could he have the painting? He kept it until his death, to her a greater compliment than sweet words. Today this painting, called *Girl Arranging*

Her Hair, is considered among Mary's best.

The work of all artists changes gradually in time, and Mary's was no exception. She had progressed from paintings of brilliant light and shadow contrasts, to the light-flooded canvases of impressionism, and in her mature years, on to works of strong compositions and well-molded forms. Now, just when she was at the height of her artistic powers, an event occurred that influenced the most important prints and paintings of her career.

Mary Cassatt, Girl Arranging Her Hair.

The influence came from far-off Japan. In 1890 a large exhibition of Japanese color prints arrived in Paris. At the first opportunity, Mary dashed to see them. She studied the simple, strong design, the flat areas of color, and the contrasting patterns. The Japanese artists did not try to create three-dimensional space on the flat surface as European artists did. They were more interested in over-all design, contrast, and harmony.

Mary returned to the Japanese exhibit often. She studied the prints until she understood them as well as she had the old masterpieces she had copied years before. Then she decided she would try to make color prints herself. The Japanese artists used woodblocks to make their color prints, but she developed a system by which she could use her metal plates for color prints.

When she engraved her first plates, Mary tried to imitate the Japanese design. The print did not look like her other work. Because she had studied the Japanese prints so well, she had absorbed their sense of design and pattern. Her new prints combined these lessons with her own subject matter. Most of her prints show women in quiet, private moments—sealing a letter, having a dress fitted, or bathing a baby.

An opportunity to exhibit the prints came sooner than Mary expected. The old impressionist group decided to have another exhibition, but it was open only to artists born in France. Of course, this left out Mary. Durand-Ruel decided to let her have her own exhibit, what was called a "one-man" show. The show consisted of twelve color prints together with five paintings.

Mary could not resist going to Durand-Ruel's many times and standing at the end of the gallery. Everything on the walls around her was her own work. Degas seemed impressed with the prints. He paused in front of *La*

Toilette and studied the young woman washing her face in a Victorian wash basin. Mary had drawn the woman's back with only a few curved lines. Her skill at drawing had greatly improved. Degas said that he did not know a woman could draw so well.

Sadness followed this success. At the end of 1891 her father died, after being ill a short time. Now Mary was left alone with her mother, who was in fragile health because of her heart problems.

Soon after the one-man show, Mary received another honor, this time from the United States. She was invited to paint a large mural to decorate the Woman's Building at the Columbian Exposition, a world's fair in Chicago. Mary was pleased that a major work of hers would be seen in her own country. Her reputation in France was growing, but outside of a few art dealers and friends in New York and Philadelphia, few Americans had heard of Mary Cassatt.

Mary carefully planned the mural to fit the theme, "modern women." Instead of showing women with their children in their homes, Mary wanted to picture women out in the world. She sketched plans for the central panel. Young women in modern dress (which was a long flowered gown in 1893) picked fruit from a tree. The tree was a symbol for science and knowledge.

When Mary transferred the small scale drawing to the mural, size proved to be a challenge. Her studio was too small. She had a special glassed-in room built to surround the enormous canvas. A hole was dug into the ground so that the center 12½-foot panel could be lowered when she worked at the top. After a summer of daily work, it was nearly finished. She wanted to invite Degas to view it, but she feared his stinging criticism. If he found too many things wrong, she would never have the heart to finish it. Finally the mural was shipped to Chicago and then installed forty feet above the floor on the north side of the Women's Building. This, the largest work that Mary ever painted, is lost today. It was probably destroyed when the building was torn down after the fair.

Mary had scarcely rolled and shipped the mural away, when Durant-Ruel approached her. Would she give another one-man show? Despite the many months spent on the mural, she was ready and selected ninety-eight recent works for this show.

In the catalog for this second exhibit, painting number one is *The Bath,* which is judged by many to be the high point of her career. In portraying a mother bathing her child, Mary combines lessons learned from the past with her own ideas and skills. The contrast between the striped pattern of the mother's dress and the design of the rug and background is like the Japanese prints. The dark-haired figures are as real as Correggio's mothers and babies in the cathedral at Parma. Other qualities are all her own. The tenderness and trust between the mother and child are shown in the closeness of their bodies and their attention on the child's foot. Painting the baby's life-like skin and the rich patterns of the background required great skill.

Mary Cassatt's paintings were becoming well known in France. She had made enough money selling her art work to be able to buy a small chateau on a forty-five acre estate. Chateau Beaufresne became her permanent summer home; in the winter Mary and her mother continued to live in their Paris apartment. At Beaufresne Mary painted in the large studio at one side of the old three-story hunting lodge. Scent from the one thousand rosebushes planted on the grounds drifted through the

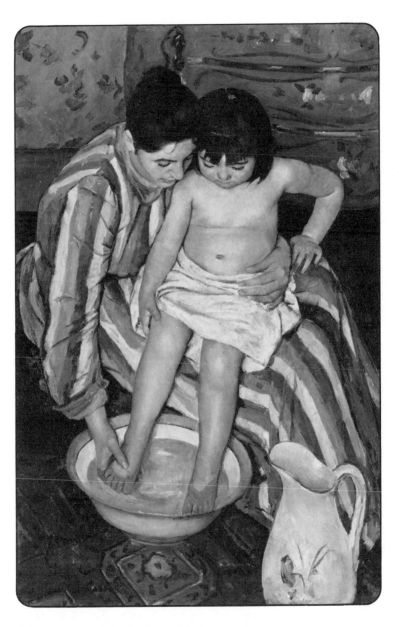

Mary Cassatt, The Bath, *c. 1891.*

tall windows. Mary always wore a simple dark skirt and white blouse to paint, although she owned dresses and suits from the finest dressmakers in Paris.

Often artists, writers, or neighbors from the village visited Chateau Beaufresne. After a morning at work, Mary joined them for lunch. Sometimes the visitors ate trout they had caught themselves in the pond. American sweet corn from the garden was served with the trout, and fruit from the orchard was dessert. After coffee Mary would return to her studio. At the age of fifty-one she enjoyed the success that her work and talent had brought.

In 1895 her mother died after suffering many years from heart disease, and Mary deeply missed the last member of her close family. The presence of Mathilde, her maid and companion, was a comfort. Each morning Mathilde brushed Mary's hair and coiled it on her head in the style of the 1890s. Mathilde managed the households at the chateau and in Paris so that Mary was free to paint.

After her mother's death and with two one-man exhibits behind her, Mary felt more free to travel. In 1898 she decided to visit Alexander and Gardner in Pennsylvania. The *Philadelphia Ledger,* in reporting her arrival, said that she was the sister of Alexander Cassatt, president of the Pennsylvania Railroad. The newspaper article went on to say that she had studied art in France and owned the smallest Pekinese dog in the world. Not a word about exhibiting with the impressionists, about the Chicago mural or her one-man shows! Actually, the newspaper did not mean to slight her; art was simply not considered very important in the United States at that time.

But soon Mary herself was to help change all that.

She began a new phase of her artistic career, one that continues to have a direct influence on art in the United States.

One of Mary's oldest friends, Louisine Havemeyer, and her husband Henry, who lived in a Fifth Avenue mansion in New York City, were collectors of art objects. When they invited Mary to go on a trip to Europe to find old masterpieces for their collection, she accepted at once. Mary thought that the United States should have fine paintings, and she knew she could help the Havemeyers find them. If old masters had hung in American museums when she was a student, she would not have needed to leave her own country.

Their treasure hunt started in Italy, where they searched for paintings from the Renaissance period. Locating the art works and then offering to buy them were delicate matters. An art dealer in Florence arranged for them to view a painting by Veronese, an Italian master. They entered a shabby palazzo that was so dark they could not see the paintings hanging against the stone walls. The owner of the painting pushed out a creaking wooden shutter. Mary looked over the paintings and found the portrait by Veronese. The painting was nearly as dirty as the walls, but it was wonderful.

Mr. Havemeyer shook his head. The woman was too full chested, and not at all beautiful. Mary insisted that the Venetians were full-busted and that they wore tight bodices. Mary, who always painted people as they were, appreciated the artist's honesty. She said that she herself would sell something to be able to buy the painting if Mr. Havemeyer refused it. Convinced, he started bargaining. Two years later the sale was completed and the Havemeyers received the Veronese in New York.

In Madrid a dealer showed Mary a painting that he claimed was done by the Spanish master Goya. Mary examined it carefully. She had studied many Goyas at the Prado museum as a young girl, and something about this Goya did not seem right. She shook her head and advised against buying. Later she learned that it was a copy of the original painting.

In Paris the Havemeyers bought modern art works, including many by Mary and by Degas.

Mary's efforts for the Havemeyers succeeded. Today most of their collection is in the Metropolitan Museum in New York and the National Gallery in Washington, D.C., where Americans can view the masterpieces they bought on the advice of Mary Cassatt.

Near the end of 1904, when she was sixty years old, Mary received the highest award of her career, the French Legion of Honor medal. The French government awards the medal only for the highest achievement in any field, and at that time it was very rare for a woman to receive the medal.

At last Mary Cassatt began to receive some recognition in the United States too. The Philadelphia Academy of Fine Arts, her old art school, awarded her its Gold Medal of Honor. Then she turned down two awards that came from the United States. Without her knowing about it, Durand-Ruel had submitted her paintings to two competitive art exhibits. The jury in each case awarded her a cash prize. But she refused the prizes and wrote careful letters to the committees, explaining that ever since she had exhibited with the impressionists, she did not believe that juries or small committees should select a few paintings for recognition. Even though the impressionists no longer exhibited, Mary remained loyal to their ideas.

Even with honors and recognition, Mary continued to paint long hours each day. Young children, alone or with their mothers, were her only subjects. During this period she seemed less interested in the unusual, strong compositions of her earlier work. She painted her mothers and children in relaxed, natural poses. The subjects speak for themselves. Still, her paintings show the developed skills of a great artist.

Mary Cassatt at the Cloisters of St. Trophime, Arles, France, in 1914.

She took particular care with one painting of a mother with her little girl and her baby. First she drew pencil sketches, then pastel studies of the figures, then the final oil painting. The painting, *Mother Looking Down, Embracing Both of Her Children,* was sold to a man in Paris, and in 1931 it was brought to the United States. Today it hangs in the White House.

In her late sixties, Mary began to have difficulty working on her prints. The glare from the metal plates bothered her eyes. The problem grew worse. When she could no longer see the fine lines, she had to give up printmaking.

Then she began to have difficulty distinguishing between some of the colors in her paintings. In 1911 she developed cataracts. She had to wait patiently until both eyes were blind before she could have surgery to restore her sight.

After her operation in 1912, she returned to pastels and worked with them for almost two years. Then again she had problems with colors. Sometimes they contrasted more harshly than she intended. Other times it was difficult to work the rounding of a cheek with gradually changing tones. Often the background was only a zigzag of chalk.

Her sight grew progressively worse, until she faced a handicap no artist can overcome. She could not see well enough to paint or draw. Partially blind, in 1914 she had to give up her art work entirely.

Events in the world at that time added to Mary's difficulties. When World War I started, Beaufresne was too close to German lines, and French authorities forced her to move to the south of France. Before leaving, her chauffeur hid her prints in the woodshed. Later German officers used Beaufresne for headquarters. Mathilde was forced to go to Switzerland because she was considered a German national, although she had spent nearly all her life in France. Without good eyesight and her companion, Mary found life in a strange villa in Grasse lonely. She wrote to friends that her dogs were a comfort.

Just before World War I ended, Degas died. Mary was in Paris at the time and attended the funeral. Sometimes he had made her extremely angry or hurt her, but she had always had deep feeling for him. She wrote to a friend that the greatest artist of the nineteenth century was gone.

Finally the war was over and Mary returned to Beaufresne. Mathilde found the prints untouched in the woodshed—only one frame had been broken. Mary lived in Beaufresne quietly for the last eight years of her life. Her health grew more frail, but her conversation and opinions remained strong and lively. She died at Beaufresne on June 14, 1926, at the age of eighty-two. Along with the rest of her family, she is buried on the grounds at Beaufresne, now a children's home.

Mary Cassatt's artistic gifts and talents live for us in her paintings. The body of her work includes 225 prints, 300 oil paintings, 400 pastels, and hundreds of water colors and drawings, an enormous output. Much of this work now hangs in the museums of the United States and of European countries, where we, too, can view the sensitive pictures of mothers and children that make up the world of Mary Cassatt.

With no formal art training, Grandma Moses became world-famous as an American primitive artist.

A Special Gift

GRANDMA MOSES

If you ask any American to name an artist, you are likely to hear, "Grandma Moses." Everyone has seen her winter scenes on Christmas cards and calendars. Her paintings of American rural life hang on the walls of major museums even more than a decade after her death. Presidents Truman, Eisenhower, and Kennedy sent her letters and cards paying tribute to her as an artist.

Yet Grandma Moses had never expressed any desire to become an artist. She never had an art lesson in her life. And she never even visited a museum until after her own work was exhibited there. In fact, she started painting when she was nearly eighty years old. For seventy-five years she had lived the life of a hard-working farm woman. Then, not wanting to be idle, she took up painting in her old age. Throughout the last twenty-five years of her life, until after her hundredth birthday, she completed nearly sixteen hundred paintings. This remarkable feat inspires young people as well as old. To have another full career after already living out one life is a triumph of the human spirit.

Grandma Moses's popularity and fame spread widely in the years following World War II. Her colorful paintings of the farm and rural life were liked and understood by everyone. In Grandma Moses's landscapes the seasons dictate the rhythm of life. Survival depends on everyone performing daily and seasonal tasks. Everyone understands exactly what chores are to be done. The confusing choices of modern life do not exist. Grandma Moses's vision of another time refreshed people and reminded them of their roots.

Another reason for her success is that even though she never studied art, she understood intuitively the principles of composition and color. Many art critics regard her use of color to indicate distance and to depict different seasons as very skilled. However, she had some difficulty in painting people and interior scenes. They are painted flat, without the perspective and shading techniques artists use to make things look three-dimensional. This flat style of painting is often called "primitive." Other terms art historians use for untaught artists who paint in this flat style are "folk" or "naive" artists.

Like Grandma Moses, most primitive artists spend their lives in isolated places without ever seeing paintings created by the trained artists of their time. Primitive artists paint for the sheer love of painting. Their work tends to have many characteristics in common with the work of young children. Never having been taught how to draw in perspective, primitive artists paint flat scenes that rely on surface pattern and decoration. Modern abstract paintings also rely on surface, two-dimensional qualities. But the modern artist makes conscious choice of contrasting shapes and colors, whereas the primitive artist is attempting to paint a scene in depth.

Paintings of primitive artists tell stories. Grandma

Moses's pictures describe life in the country, historic events—like the Battle of Bennington during the Revolutionary War—or the words of a song—like "The Old Oaken Bucket." She paints every detail of the battle and every object mentioned in the song.

Without any training in art school, almost without any education at all, Grandma Moses's preparation for the art career that brought her fame lay in her long life itself. To look at her work is to recreate her long life on her farm.

Grandma Moses was born Anna Mary Robertson on September 7, 1860, near Greenwich, New York. Her father's farm was "back in the green meadows and wild woods," as she writes in her autobiography. Anna Mary, the third oldest in a family of ten children, spent the first twelve years of her life on this farm. She describes these years as a carefree, happy time. But they were busy years, for the children were expected to help the family with chores. Farm and household duties filled each day from sun-up until candlelight. On Sundays the family took time off to take a walk. She remembers that her father always carried the baby. Going to church was one of the few other entertainments, but the Robertsons lived too far back in the country to go to church every Sunday.

Another diversion was storytelling. Like most children, Anna Mary loved to hear about her ancestors. She remembered stories that her grandaunt Celina King told about her father, Hezekiah King. He came to the Cambridge Valley in about 1775, cleared a farm out of the wilderness, and built a sturdy, gray shingled house. Although she never saw this house because it had burned in 1800, Grandma Moses later painted it several times. Aunt Celina King had described the thick walls and sturdy structure so thoroughly that Grandma Moses could picture it in her mind and then in her paintings, many years after she heard the stories.

The farm of her own childhood appears in many paintings. She always included the house, barns, and the flax mill that her father operated. The barns occupy a prominent, central part of the painting, surrounded by wagons, animals, tiny figures, and the orchard and fields.

Since the Robertson children had no toys or dolls bought in the store, Anna Mary used to cut rows of paper dolls. Using some of her mother's supply of indigo, a substance added to rinse water on wash day, she painted blue eyes. If she could find grape juice, she used that for the lips. The paper dolls had corsets, scalloped petticoats, and dresses with three flounces. She loved to create dresses out of colored paper and white doilies. Once, when Grandma Robertson brought her some pink and green tissue paper, Anna Mary felt very rich indeed.

Other times during her childhood, her father bought sheets of paper used for newspapers, for a penny each. Anna Mary and her brothers loved to draw, using berries or grapes for paint. These drawings were her first art work. Later her father gave her some paint, left over after he had painted scenes of Lake George on the wall. But she did not have any paper then, so she painted on pieces of slate and windowpanes. Her father liked to see her paint, but her brothers made fun of her brilliant "lambscapes." Her mother thought that Anna Mary should spend her time in more useful ways.

Each season on the Robertson farm brought its share of chores. A cow or steer was slaughtered each winter. Women canned the beef to provide meat for the following summer, and they melted tallow, or waste fat, to make candles. The liquid tallow was poured into candle molds that had been threaded with wicking, a heavy string. As soon as the candles hardened, they were pulled out of the molds. Many years later, Grandma Moses painted two women making candles in *Candle Dip Day in 1800.*

One of the early spring chores turned into a holiday for the children. This was sugaring off, when maple sap was tapped, then boiled down to make syrup and sugar. Grandma Moses's scenes of sugaring off are among her best paintings. The background is always a snowy winter landscape. Bare-branched maple trees with a tapping pail strapped to their trunks reach from the ground to the sky. Yoked oxen pull sleds loaded with barrels of sap, and a large pot of boiling sap sits over a ring of red flames. Figures in the painting tend the boiling syrup and pour the "wax" into barrels of snow to harden into maple sugar. The children wait anxiously for bowls of

Grandma Moses, Sugaring Time, *1954.*

snow topped with thick, warm maple syrup. Grandma Moses remembers having a happy time eating this treat, and then going home to "dream sweet dreams."

One of her earliest memories was of a trip in the buggy to visit her grandmother on a spring day. As they approached the village of Cambridge, they saw black bunting wrapped around the posts on the porch of the store. Her mother asked about the black trim and was told that President Abraham Lincoln had been shot. Grandma Moses carried the memory for nearly one hundred years. In a painting called *Lincoln,* she painted a village with the door frames wrapped in black bunting.

When Anna Mary was twelve years old, her childhood ended abruptly; she went to work as a hired girl. Although she was well treated by the families she served, she felt that she stopped being carefree and young when she left home. She first worked for the Whiteside family. On Sundays, after she fixed breakfast and fed the chickens, she hitched up Old Black Joe and drove the Whitesides to church. Built by Mr. Whiteside's ancestors, the church was crowded to the last pew on Sundays. Grandma Moses remembered the vertical boards and windows and later painted the white church and its cemetery.

After leaving the Whitesides, Anna Mary worked for the Vandenbergs, who lived at Eagle Bridge. While working for them, she attended the one-room school when it was in session, usually for three months during the winter and three during the summer. She had rarely gone to school while she had lived at home. In those days, it was not considered important for a girl to go to school. Education was at home, learning the skills of keeping a house and rearing a large family of ten or twelve children. But Anna Mary liked the Eagle Bridge school. Later her children, grandchildren, and great-

Anna Mary Robertson at the age of eighteen.

grandchildren attended this one-room school after Anna Mary settled with her own family on the farm next to the Vandenbergs.

Later, she worked for a family named Burch. One day she and Mrs. Burch took a drink from the well. When Anna Mary pulled up the wooden bucket, Mrs. Burch told her that this well had inspired the song "The Old Oaken Bucket." One of Mrs. Burch's ancestors had written the words for the song while working out at sea. Grandma Moses always remembered the story and the farm when she heard the song. She painted the wooden bucket, the well, and the farm buildings many times.

In the fall of 1886 she went to work for the James family. There she met Thomas Moses, who worked on the same farm. Gradually they became acquainted. He learned that she was a good cook; she learned that he was from a good family. In those days, she later said, women looked for a man with a good reputation; a rich man lasted only as long as his pocketbook.

The following year, on November 9, 1887, she and Thomas Moses were married. Thomas had decided to take a job on a horse ranch in North Carolina, and they started the journey on a train bound for New York City. This was Anna Mary's first experience away from the familiar valleys and hills of Washington County. Instead of sleeping on the train, they left it to spend the night in hotels and boarding houses along the way. In Staunton, Virginia, they were persuaded to stay in the Shenandoah Valley and take over a farm from a family who did not like working the soil.

Soon after they settled on the farm, Anna Mary Moses sent some of her home-churned butter to the store to trade for other supplies. The storekeeper tasted her Yankee butter and declared it delicious. He gave her twelve cents a pound in trade. The next time she brought some in, he raised the price to fifteen cents, then twenty. Less than a year after they came to Virginia, Anna Mary's Yankee butter had paid for the two cows that she and Thomas had bought. She felt pride at doing her share to support them.

In October, 1888, the storekeeper offered them a six-hundred-acre dairy farm if Anna Mary would supply him with all the butter she could churn from the milk given by the herd of cows. They agreed to move. Anna Mary churned butter twice each day in a dairy room that had running water, a luxury to her. Each week she shipped two crates of butter to a hotel at White Sulphur Springs, West Virginia.

While she churned the heavy barrel churn, she looked many miles down the beautiful Shenandoah Valley. She loved to watch the smoke from steam trains puffing out against the Blue Ridge Mountains and wished she could paint a picture of it. Many years later, Grandma Moses did paint several scenes of the Shenandoah Valley.

Not long after they moved to the dairy farm. her first child, Winona Moses, was born, on December 2, 1888. Then three years later on the same day, a son, Loyd, was born. Even with the added care of two young children, Anna Mary continued to ship out two crates of butter each week.

When Loyd was only a baby, the Moses family moved to another farm, called the Dudley place. The large, two-story, red brick farmhouse appears in Grandma Moses's painting, *Apple Butter Making*. In the center of the painting, a bubbling brass pot of apple butter hangs over the open fire. People pick apples, peel apples, and cut logs for the fire. In the foreground, there is a tiny figure in a mauve dress, who is Grandma Moses. She carries a pail and is probably going for sugar to add to the apple butter. Grandma Moses gives the recipe for apple butter in her autobiography. They started with two barrels of apple cider, added three barrels of quartered, peeled apples, then cooked and stirred this mixture until midnight. Sweetened with twenty pounds of sugar, the apple butter yielded forty gallons. All of that apple butter sweetened the biscuits of the family and hungry work crews throughout the winter when fresh fruit was not available.

Another son, Forrest, was born at the Dudley place, and then a daughter, Anna. Anna Mary no longer made butter at the Dudley place, but she washed sixty to one hundred milk bottles each day by hand, for Thomas to use to deliver milk to his customers. By now the older children were helping Anna Mary with the chores, just as she had helped her mother.

The years of hard work on the farms rewarded them, for after eight years on the Dudley place, they were able to buy their own farm, Mount Airy. In later years Grandma Moses painted Mount Airy's stone farmhouse, barns, and fields. Here her last child, Hugh, was born. After only two years at Mount Airy, Thomas decided to sell the farm. He had always missed the Hoosick River Valley, his New York home; he longed to return. But it was fall, and Anna Mary knew that she had to sew heavy clothes to protect five children from the cold New York winter. Thomas found a small farm, Mount Nebo, for them to use temporarily while Anna Mary prepared the family for the return to the cold climate. The stay stretched to two years. Never one to be idle, Anna Mary made potato chips, slicing and frying them herself. They were shipped to White Sulphur Springs, as her butter had been. Then after two years, with warm clothes stitched for the whole family, they left the Shenandoah Valley.

Grandma Moses later painted the return to New York in *Moving Day on the Farm*. Caged chickens, baskets of apples, and piles of pumpkins sit ready to be stacked on the open farm wagon.

Soon after settling onto the Eagle Bridge farm, which the children named Mount Nebo, Thomas bought a herd of cows and returned to bottling and selling milk. Anna Mary painted and papered the entire house in addition to doing her daily chores. Monday was washday, Tuesday ironing, Wednesday baking and cleaning, Thursday sewing, and Friday garden work and leftover jobs. Only the seasons changed chores. Spring brought sugaring off, followed by planting. In summer hungry haying and threshing crews had to be fed. Berries and other fruits ripened for canning. Fall brought apples for pressing into cider. Winter meant attention to indoor repairs and sewing.

The seasons also brought their share of fun. Grandma Moses wrote that children eagerly waited all year long for the church picnic, when they could eat all the cake, lemonade, watermelon, and peanuts they could hold. In *Picnic* she painted the children playing ball and swinging from a long tree swing. The table, laden with food, stands out in white at the center of the painting as does the white New England church behind it.

Although the rhythm of country life repeated year after year, time brought slow changes. The children were growing and striking out on their own. The oldest, Winona, went to business school in Albany not long after the family moved to Eagle Bridge. Loyd and Forrest attended agriculture schools and returned to run a sheep farm Thomas and Anna Mary had bought for them. Losses, like the death of Anna Mary's parents in 1909, changed and saddened life.

New inventions began to affect farm life, often making it easier and speeding up the pace. In 1907, Anna Mary saw the first balloon floating between Argyle and Cambridge. This balloon floats over the green Cambridge Valley in a painting she did fifty years later. In 1913 electric lights appeared in Albany, but not on the farm until 1936.

In 1913 the Moses family bought their first car, an Overland. But Anna Mary preferred horses and drove around the countryside in a surrey. One day, she was sitting alone in the surrey while her sister tried to hitch

Topsy, the horse. Topsy balked and ran, covering two miles before spilling Anna Mary out into a slimy pond. Even though she broke an arm and was badly bruised in the fall, she later painted Topsy several times, always quietly hitched to a buggy or peacefully grazing.

In 1918, she again wallpapered the house. But she ran out of paper before covering the fireboard. She pasted plain paper over the board and then painted a scene with a lake on it. She wanted to picture the lake in the sunlight, so she painted the water yellow, showing her understanding of reflected sunlight. A few years later, when she papered the room again, she had enough to cover the fireboard and papered over her painting without a moment's hesitation. But after she became famous, her daughter-in-law suggested that they strip off the wallpaper. The old painting was still there, although a bit faded.

About 1920 her desire to decorate things or "to make them pretty" again inspired her to paint the side panels of her "tip-up" table. The pine board table, made in 1762, contained storage boxes for pewter ware. Anna Mary used the table for a flower stand. Then, after she began to paint, it became her easel. She painted hundreds of pictures on it.

By 1927 both of the youngest children, Anna and Hugh, had married. Hugh and his wife Dorothy lived with Thomas and Anna Mary, taking over more of the farm work as the parents grew older. One bitterly cold January day, Thomas complained of the cold and was unable to carry in wood for the stove. That night he died of a heart attack. Anna Mary grieved over the death of her husband of nearly forty years, but she accepted the grief, as she accepted the seasons of the year. Both grief and joy fit into the natural order of things, as do howling winter blizzards and warm spring days. Later she accepted her fame and success as an artist in the same way. It was simply part of the natural order.

When her daughter Anna became ill in 1930, Anna Mary went to nearby Bennington, Vermont, to care for her and the two children. Two years later Anna died of a lung hemorrhage. Anna Mary stayed on, caring for her daughter's husband and children. After the meals were cooked and cleaned up, the clothes washed, and the canning done, Grandma Moses, now in her seventies, picked up pieces of linen and stitched "worsted" pictures. She drew a design on the cloth and then embroidered the picture solidly into every inch of cloth with different colors of yarn. She embroidered some scenes from books and postcards. Others, like her Eagle Bridge farm, were taken from memory. She loved stitching the "fancy work," as she called the pictures, even though sometimes her finger joints ached with arthritis. Her solution to the pains of aging was simply to stay active.

When Anna's husband remarried in 1935, Grandma Moses returned to Mount Nebo. Hugh and Dorothy continued to care for the farm and house, as they had done in Grandma Moses's absence. Grandma Moses stayed busy with more of the yarn pictures, in spite of increasing stiffness in her fingers. She sold some and gave others away. When one of her sisters, Celestia, saw her laboriously embroidering an entire picture, she suggested that Grandma Moses could paint pictures faster and better. Grandma Moses agreed to try. She found some paint in the barn and some canvas used for mending the cover for a farm machine. After cutting a square from the canvas, she painted a small landscape with cows, a scene she had previously stitched into a "worsted" picture. Then she painted more scenes she had seen on postcards or in books. When the paint she had found in the barn ran out, she ordered artist's supplies from the Sears, Roebuck catalog. She entered the paintings in the county fair, along with her canned fruit and raspberry jam. She won prizes only for her preserves, while the paintings remained unnoticed. But, after all, she had perfected techniques for making jam over a lifetime; she had been painting only a few months.

After she had a few paintings on hand, Hugh and Dorothy took them to the Woman's Exchange in the Thomas Drug Store in Hoosick Falls. There farm women sold things they had made with their hands. Some of the paintings Grandma Moses had to display were the scenes she copied from illustrations. But as she became more sure of her skill, she stopped copying scenes and painted from her own memories. Sugaring off pictures were among the earliest. They are much more successful than the copied scenes because she is painting an experience as well as a pretty scene. These paintings are far more interesting than the earlier works, because they show the beginnings of her own style.

On Easter Sunday of 1938, Louis Calder, an engineer and art collector from New York City, saw Grandma Moses's paintings in the drug store window. Amazed and impressed with the fresh style of this untaught artist, he bought all the paintings. Asking about the artist, he was directed to her farm. She was not at home, but Dorothy told him that she had ten more paintings to sell. When Grandma Moses returned home that night, she found only nine paintings. Not wanting to disappoint the buyer, she cut one of the larger scenes of the Shenandoah Valley in half and put each half into two smaller frames. She now had the promised ten. Calder returned the following day and bought them.

He continued to be interested in her work, making several trips to Eagle Bridge to collect more of the paintings. In New York he showed them to gallery owners and museum curators. Many people felt that they were interesting primitive art, but because they were so different from the modern art of that period, no one wanted to exhibit them. Then in 1939, Sidney Janis, who later owned a famous gallery in New York, selected three Grandma Moses paintings to be part of an exhibit of contemporary unknown American painters at the Museum of Modern Art. It was her first exhibit in New York at a major museum. She was nearly eighty years old, and she had been painting only a few years.

Not long after the exhibit at the Museum of Modern Art, Louis Calder took the paintings to Otto Kallir, a dealer with galleries in Paris and Vienna. Kallir was opening a New York branch called Galerie St. Etienne. Keenly interested in primitive art, Kallir thought some of the paintings were excellent and agreed to exhibit them. He selected thirty-four paintings and arranged them in Grandma Moses's first "one-man" exhibit, entitled, "What a Farm Wife Painted." Most people who viewed the exhibit liked the scenes of farm life immediately. Newspaper reviews were favorable. Most important of all, Otto Kallir became Grandma Moses's dealer, close friend, promoter, and protector for the rest of her life. He asked her to the opening, but she turned down the invitation, saying that she already knew the paintings.

A few weeks later she did make the trip to the city, to Gimbel's department store, where these paintings were exhibited in the auditorium at a Thanksgiving festival. Carolyn Thomas, wife of the drug store owner in Hoosick Falls, accompanied her to New York. The city confused Grandma Moses. She had not been there since she went through in 1905 on the return trip from Virginia. At Gimbel's someone clipped something around her neck that she thought looked like a black bug but turned out to be a microphone. When Grandma Moses thought she was talking to only one person, she spoke to four hundred people in Gimbel's auditorium. She talked about the preserves she had brought. She told how to make them and offered samples to the people. Although she made several other trips to New York City as her fame grew, she never felt comfortable there.

After her paintings were exhibited, she seemed to gain more confidence in her work. The size of her paintings increased, and the scenes became more complicated. The New York exhibit also brought more sales.

In 1942 Grandma Moses had two "one-man" exhibits. Ala Story, director of the American British Art Center, became interested in her work and exhibited Grandma Moses's paintings at the art center. One painting, *Black Horses,* shows the rapid progress the artist had made. Her work before this time had been charming and appealing primitive art, but *Black Horses* demonstrates her skilled mastery of landscape painting. The scene looks over a large expanse of the Cambridge Valley. The fields look like patchwork, in pale, well-coordinated colors that indicate vast distance. Trees in the foreground give a sense of depth and unity to the scene; two groups of horses, one on each side of the painting, balance each other. The black horses on the right belonged to Grandma Moses's great-grandfather, Hezekiah King, who fought in the Revolution. Most of the human figures and animals in the paintings were specific people and animals, and Grandma Moses could tell stories about them.

During the World War II years, Grandma Moses

had several exhibits throughout the country as well as shows at Galerie St. Etienne and the American British Art Center in New York. Many people who viewed the paintings liked them so well they wrote to Grandma Moses and requested her to paint a certain scene for them. Even though she did not really like to repeat the paintings, she wanted to satisfy people. She repeated scenes, but she made each painting a little different in composition. She once said that she pretended the scene lay just outside her window. Sometimes she looked at it from the right, and other times she painted it from the left. She changed the seasons, but she kept the barns, houses, or mills of the original scene. These requests explain the repetition of her most popular themes.

Among her best known paintings were those of a checkered house. As a child Grandma Moses actually

Grandma Moses, Black Horses, *c. 1942.*

saw this incredible house, which stood like a giant vertical chess board near Cambridge, New York. At one
time it had served as Revolutionary War headquarters
for General Baum, and later it became a stagecoach
stop. Paintings of the checkered house are done in the
style that became associated with her work. The house
is set in the rolling countryside. Sometimes the hills are
pale spring-green, sometimes snow covered. The decorative red and white checkered house is set in the center of
the painting, surrounded by barns, carriages, and tiny
figures. The background landscape shows her skill in
capturing great distance and her understanding of perspective. Her colors are well chosen to represent seasons.
By contrast, the foreground figures are flat, painted
without accurate proportions in a childlike primitive
style. This combination of well-executed landscapes with
flat, primitive figures is known as the Grandma Moses
style. People all over the world have learned to recognize
and love this style.

During the late 1940s, the size of some of her paintings increased from their usual eighteen by twenty-four
inches to thirty-six by forty-eight inches. The larger
paintings are not merely enlarged versions of the smaller
paintings; they show more activity and more complicated
composition. *Country Fair* presents an entire village,
set in the soft green summer countryside, filled with the
activity of fair day. Horses and buggies dash to the fair
on roads leading into town. There is a Ferris wheel, a
merry-go-round, a balloon man, and various sizes and
shapes of horse-drawn trams and buggies. Cows, lambs,
chickens, and pigs fill the lower part of the painting.
Country Fair can be studied many times, and each time
some previously unnoticed figure can be discovered.
Perhaps it is the mother bending over the baby carriage

or the three boys sitting on the barn stall railing. The large paintings were too big for Grandma Moses's tip-up table and had to be painted propped on her bed. Eventually they became physically too taxing for her, and she stopped painting this size after 1950.

Grandma Moses's paintings reached an even wider audience when the Hallmark Company began to reproduce her scenes on greeting cards. One of the most famous, *Out for Christmas Trees,* was reproduced many times. This painting not only inspires longing for the time when a family could go out into the woods to cut their Christmas tree, it also is among Grandma Moses's finest. Dark green fir trees contrast with the white snow. Horses pull sleighs and Christmas trees toward the house at the bottom left. Smoke rises from the chimney of the house, and the multi-paned windows are pulled shut. It is easy to imagine the snug rooms and open fires inside.

Grandma Moses had lived through many crisp, snowy winter days. Someone once suggested that she paint shadows on the snow blue. She claimed that as many times as she had looked at the snow, she never had seen any blue. She thought the shadows were gray and she painted them that way. She also sprinkled mica glitter on the wet white paint to represent glistening sunlight on the snow. She tried to paint things exactly as she saw them.

In May 1949, she traveled to Washington, D.C., to receive the Women's National Press Club award for her outstanding accomplishment in the field of art. Six women, including Eleanor Roosevelt, were awarded the honor for contributions to their various fields. President Harry Truman presented the awards.

Later, Otto Kallir donated one of her paintings to the Trumans for the President's mansion. *July Fourth,* showing an old-fashioned parade and Independence Day celebration, hangs in the White House today.

European recognition of Grandma Moses came in 1950, when the U.S. Information Agency organized a large exhibit of her paintings that traveled to major cities throughout Europe. Later her work was included in a European tour, sponsored by the Smithsonian Institution, of American primitive artists. Europeans viewed her scenes of rural life with the same interest and warmth that Americans did.

In March 1952, General Dwight D. Eisenhower sent her a greeting card with a reproduction of one of his amateur paintings. He inscribed it, "to a real artist." In 1955 she painted, from color photographs, two scenes of the Eisenhowers' Gettysburg farm. The President's Cabinet selected one of the paintings and presented it to him as a gift on the third anniversary of his inauguration.

Even though Grandma Moses had achieved recognition by two presidents, had attracted a following in Europe, and had earned a great deal of money from the sale of her work, she did not simply keep repeating the same type of paintings that had made her famous. Now in her early nineties, she tried new things. A neighbor brought her some ceramic tiles, and she painted scenes on these. Usually she painted one house, a tree, or a covered bridge—selecting simple elements from her paintings that were suitable for the six-by-six-inch surface of the tile.

As her fame spread, people loved to hear stories about her remarkable accomplishments and about events in her long life. In 1946 she had written some comments about her work that were published with reproductions of her paintings and an essay by Otto Kallir in *Grandma*

Grandma Moses, Rainbow, *1961.*

Grandma Moses with two of her great-grandchildren in 1949.

Moses, American Primitive. In the early 1950s, Kallir encouraged her to write down more of her experiences. She filled 169 handwritten pages with anecdotes from her childhood on through her long life. She was as skilled at creating word pictures as she was in painting scenes. These memories were published in the book *Grandma Moses: My Life's History.*

She also began to paint indoor scenes. Unable to use a landscape for background, Grandma Moses painted the indoor scenes in more of the flat, decorative quality of primitive art. Large rooms filled with family activity at Christmas and Thanksgiving are painted in warm colors.

Two of her most interesting interior scenes depict quilting bees. The colorful patchwork quilts themselves dominate the paintings. Activity centers around the quilt and around tables that are filled with food. Dogs and children scamper underfoot.

In 1955 Grandma Moses agreed to be interviewed and to paint a picture on television. Over a period of several days she painted a *Sugaring Off* scene in front of the television cameras. The film was edited and then presented on Edward R. Murrow's program entitled, "See It Now," along with the interview. After he had asked her only a few questions, Grandma Moses put some paper in front of Edward R. Murrow and asked him to draw something. When he claimed that he could not draw, she said that anybody could paint; there was nothing to it at all. She herself had this attitude about her own painting. She did not regard it as a special gift but said it was just like "fancy work."

In general, she refused to paint subjects that she was not familiar with herself. However, she did illustrate some children's stories, and she painted a series of scenes to illustrate *The Night before Christmas.* She knew the poem by heart and she seemed to especially enjoy doing these paintings. One of this series, called *So Long Till Next Year,* is among her finest paintings, although it was not used in the book. A white moon in a deep blue midnight sky gives an ordinary night scene a magic atmosphere. Feathery, bare branches of trees and a board house are bathed in the white moonlight. Santa and his reindeer ride through this magic blue landscape that exists in the Christmas Eve dreams of young children.

The painting of the scenes for *The Night before Christmas* was interrupted by the celebration for her hundredth birthday. Greetings came from Presidents Truman and Eisenhower. Governor Nelson Rockefeller proclaimed September 7, 1960, as Grandma Moses Day in New York. Her sons, Loyd and Forrest, held a week-long open house where she sat, serene and untroubled, receiving her visitors.

After the celebration ended, she again picked up her brushes. As the year progressed, she worked almost every day, but her hand was less steady now. When she dotted in the eyes or added other details, she rested her right hand over her left to steady the brush. Then her strength ebbed, and details smudged into almost impressionistic areas of color. In June of 1961 she painted her last painting. A rainbow arches over the summer fields of the Cambridge Valley. She could not have chosen a better symbol of hope to end a productive career and life that had lasted more than a century. She died on December 13, 1961.

Grandma Moses had lived two lives. The first, as a hard-working farm woman, was shared with her family. The second, as an artist, was shared with all who enjoyed her paintings. What a rich gift she gave us all!

Georgia O'Keeffe's art has been strongly influenced by her love for the countryside of New Mexico.

A Unique Vision

GEORGIA O'KEEFFE

In the early summer of 1929 artist Georgia O'Keeffe traveled from her home in New York City to Taos, New Mexico. When she reached New Mexico, her artist's eye studied every detail of the mesas, the high desert tablelands. Deep canyons cut into the mesas and emptied onto the desert floor hundreds of feet below. Bright sunlight exposed every peak and valley of the Sangre de Cristo mountains near Taos. The earth looked as naked as a skeleton, without a leafy tree or a single blade of grass to cover it. "Wonderful!" she exclaimed. "No one told me it was like this!" Those words were on her lips many times that summer.

Georgia O'Keeffe, then forty-one years old, had already earned fame as an artist. Her paintings were exhibited regularly in New York galleries. Articles about these exhibits appeared in New York newspapers, and art critics wrote about her work in art magazines. She was well known for her large paintings of flowers. She would often cover an entire canvas with a single blossom. One painting of an enormous lily had sold for several thousand dollars in 1927, at that time a record price for a painting done by a living American artist.

Mabel Dodge, a supporter of artists and writers, had invited Georgia O'Keeffe to spend that summer in Taos. Mabel had built a cluster of earth-colored adobe buildings at the base of Taos Mountain, and she hoped that artists would come there to paint in the clear light of New Mexico during the day. In the evenings they could discuss their work and ideas.

The desert landscape excited Georgia O'Keeffe, and she enjoyed taking walks by herself behind the adobe buildings. Often, after a walk, she got out a freshly stretched canvas and painted the landscape. She never painted details as a camera might photograph desert rocks, but she recorded the landscape in simple, strong shapes and bright bands of color. The base of one painting is a band of gray green, representing piñon and juniper trees. Beyond the trees rise the pink cliffs of mesas, then the indigo and violet of distant mountains. Her colors look as if she had mixed the clay and sand of the desert with oil and put them on the canvas. Her rock formations and mountains appear in shapes as bold as the windswept landscape.

During the evening discussions with other artists, Georgia O'Keeffe heard stories about the early Spanish settlers, who came to this region in the early 1600s. Some of the Spanish settlers belonged to religious sects called Penitentes. They beat themselves or punished themselves in other painful ways in order to imitate the suffering of Jesus on the cross. These harsh religious practices inspired Georgia O'Keeffe to fill one of her canvases with an enormous, heavy black cross that seems to burst out of the edge of the painting. Behind the cross, desert hills stretch in row upon row to a crimson horizon.

When the cross painting was later exhibited in New York, some people were shocked. What did it mean? Georgia O'Keeffe answered that anyone who did not feel that cross did not understand the country. The desert was as harsh as the religious rituals of the Penitentes, who beat themselves to ask forgiveness for their sins.

Georgia O'Keeffe, Black Cross, New Mexico, *1929.*

That summer in Taos changed Georgia O'Keeffe's art and her life forever. Instead of painting New York skyscrapers, she painted mountains and mesas. After 1929 she spent nearly every summer in New Mexico. Eventually she settled there permanently, and she still lives in Abiquiu, where she has an adobe house in the village and a ranch house about twenty miles away in an isolated portion of the desert.

The badlands surrounding her ranch near Abiquiu are a contrast to the gentle Wisconsin countryside where Georgia O'Keeffe was born on November 15, 1887. The white board farm house of the O'Keeffe dairy farm was a lively place, filled with Georgia's parents, seven children, Great-aunt Jenny Varney, and the schoolteacher who boarded with the O'Keeffes. The Town Hall school was just across the road.

Young Georgia, the second oldest, always loved to draw. In the one-room Town Hall school, she used all her spare time to draw and covered many papers with her pictures. She gave some of them to her seat-mate, who still owns them. By the time she was ten, Georgia had decided that she would be an artist.

After dark in the farm house, Georgia's mother often read to the children. In the kerosene lamplight Georgia listened to stories from history and tales of the wild west. The western stories were her favorite, and she could not forget them. On many nights, long after she went to bed, she tried to imagine pioneers riding in covered wagons over the dusty trails of the plains and desert. Outside Georgia's window, the Wisconsin farm fields were as orderly as the neat pieces of a patchwork quilt. She was sure the West was different. How could fences or roads march across the rugged canyons and mountains in straight, crisscrossing patterns? Life in the West, too, had to be filled with more surprises and dangers than the orderly pattern of dairy farming. Georgia carried this impression of the West with her until she saw that area for herself many years later.

When Georgia entered high school, she went to Sacred Heart Academy, a Dominican convent in nearby Madison, Wisconsin. At the academy, Georgia took watercolor painting in addition to the regular subjects of arithmetic, reading, and science. The nun who taught the art class recognized Georgia's talent. She also noticed that her pupil drew everything very small, and one day she asked Georgia about it.

To tease the teacher, Georgia found a piece of paper a yard square and filled it with one enormous poppy. While this poppy was a joke, years later she became famous for painting single, enormous flowers. From this time on in the watercolor class, Georgia drew everything on a larger scale.

Georgia attended Sacred Heart Academy through the ninth grade. Then she went to Central High School in Madison. In 1902 she joined her family in Williamsburg, Virginia, where they had moved. During the winter, Georgia went to boarding school at Chatham Episcopal Institute at Chatham, Virginia. Sometimes she did not work very well at this school, but other times she worked very hard. One of her teachers at Chatham thought she was very talented. Years later, when Georgia O'Keeffe was a well-known artist, the teacher came to see all of her exhibits.

When she was sixteen years old, Georgia graduated from Chatham Institute. She knew that she wanted to go to a professional art school, where she would find the training she needed to become an artist, and she chose the Chicago Art Institute. There John

Vanderpoel taught her drawing and anatomy. She was learning techniques, how to draw things accurately as she saw them. But before the school year was over, she caught typhoid fever and became very ill. She returned to Williamsburg, where she spent a whole year recovering at home.

Afterwards, Georgia was ready to return to art school, and decided to try a different one, the Art Students League in New York. On the first day of classes, Georgia had just settled into her chair in a painting class when, quite dramatically, the instructor, William Chase, entered the room. He wore a tall silk hat, light spats, and gloves. Since Georgia was used to seeing country people in Wisconsin and Virginia, she was very impressed.

William Chase told his students to use rich pigments, with some areas of the painting highlighted and others deeply shadowed. He awed the students with a demonstration of completing a figure study in only three hours. He painted with rapid, slashing brush strokes. His favorite subjects were still lifes, often a dead fish or game bird beside a shadowed cooking pot.

At the end of the school year Georgia O'Keeffe painted a dead rabbit beside a copper pot. She must have learned her lessons from William Chase well, for the painting won a Chase Still Life Scholarship. The prize money provided funds for study that summer at the Art Students League Outdoor School at Lake George in upstate New York.

When she returned to Virginia at the end of the summer and looked at the paintings and drawings she had done that year, Georgia was discouraged. They all looked like things the teachers had done and were no better than hundreds and hundreds of other paintings. Actually, she thought they were not as good as many.

Why repeat what had already been done? So she destroyed every bit of her art work and gave up the idea of being a fine artist, trying to create original paintings that would hang in museums and art galleries.

Still, at twenty-one, she needed to support herself, and drawing was her best skill. She took a job as a commercial illustrator in Chicago, drawing lace and embroidery for advertisements. But again illness interrupted her plans. She caught measles, and the disease affected her eyesight. She was no longer able to do close, exacting drawing, and she had to quit her job. Again discouraged, she returned to her family in Virginia.

The O'Keeffes had now moved to Charlottesville, where the University of Virginia is located. One of Georgia's sisters asked her to attend a summer art class at the university. At first Georgia was reluctant, but finally she went to a class taught by Alon Bement. After sitting in only once or twice, she decided to enroll.

Bement's ideas offered Georgia fresh vision and insight. He believed that a painting should not try to reproduce the way something else looked but should be a design in itself. The design should be based on flat patterns and simple lines. These were the artistic principles of the Japanese prints that had influenced Mary Cassatt.

After Georgia had been in the art class only two weeks, Bement invited her to teach the following summer at the University of Virginia. But first she needed to have some teaching experience. Almost by magic, it seemed, a telegram arrived informing her she had been accepted as an art supervisor in the public schools in Amarillo, Texas.

In the fall of 1914, when she boarded the train for Amarillo, she remembered the wild west stories her mother had read to her. In only hours she would see for herself. When she arrived on the flat, windswept plains of west Texas, her excitement was intense. She felt that here was where she belonged. Only a few spindly maples and ragweed grew; there was not a tree trunk bigger than six inches around and no flowers for her pupils to paint. "But I was absolutely crazy about it," she said years later in an interview with Katherine Kuh. "That was my country—terrible winds and a wonderful emptiness." And the job fulfilled the teaching requirement for the University of Virginia, where she taught the following two summers.

After the University of Virginia summer session of 1915, Alon Bement urged Georgia to go to Columbia University in New York City to study with Arthur Dow. Arthur Dow's ideas had inspired the principles of design and simplicity that Bement taught his students. Georgia O'Keeffe had already mastered techniques of using oil and watercolors. Then "Arthur Dow gave me something to do with them," she later said. "This man had one dominating idea: to fill a space in a beautiful way."

In her art classes at Columbia, Georgia and another student, Anita Pollitzer, were separated by a screen from the other art students. Arthur Dow allowed them to paint still lifes and flower studies, while the other students had to draw from plaster casts. Georgia painted with the brightest colors, the cleanest palette, and the best brushes. She had to do without other things to buy these fine supplies, Anita Pollitzer remembers. She also worked very hard. She adored dancing, but she refused invitations to go out dancing at night because that took time away from her art. She lived in a simple, white-walled bedroom. The only decoration was a pot of red geraniums on the fire escape.

After one year at Columbia University, Georgia decided that she wanted to have more time to paint on her own and accepted a job teaching at Columbia College in Columbia, South Carolina. Away from her intense studies and the ideas of a teacher, she felt it was time to look back over her work and measure where she stood as an artist. She closed herself in her room and set out all the oil paintings, watercolors, and drawings of the past three years. Slowly she studied each art work at this private exhibition. She saw the influence of Alon Bement from Virginia, and even William Chase and John Vanderpoel from her first years of study. The most prominent influence was her most recent teacher, Arthur Dow.

She was dissatisfied. The art ought to be her own. Other things in her life were tied to her need to earn money: she had to live where she could get a job, she had to teach what was expected by the schools, she even had to dress and behave in a way proper for a teacher. But she did not have to paint to please anyone else. She had things in her head that no one else had told her to put down, or that no other artists had ever painted. She was a fool not to let her art be whatever she wanted to paint or draw.

She took out a fresh sheet of paper and a piece of charcoal and began to draw in swirls and rhythms. Shapes repeated themselves like a haunting melody. Sometimes a jagged, bold streak raced upward on the paper like a bolt of lightning. Other times a simple, spare line cut the paper. These were things she saw and even heard in her own mind. They were entirely her own.

Georgia rolled up her drawings and sent them to Anita Pollitzer. But she wrote a warning: They must not be shown to anyone. They were meant only to be seen by Georgia's closest friend.

When Anita Pollitzer pulled the package from her Columbia University post office box, she knew it contained new drawings. She hurried to the college studio, locked the door, and spread the papers on the floor. She had never seen anything like these drawings before. They were exciting, alive patterns. She felt this new vision had to be shared, even if it displeased Georgia. She rolled them up again, stuck them under her arm, and carried them, through the rain, to 291, a gallery at 291 Fifth Avenue.

Gallery 291 was a special place in those days. Alfred Stieglitz, the owner, was a famous photographer who also operated the art gallery. He was the first person who dared to show works of modern art in New York. He thought it was very important that unusual, new expressions in art be exposed. The paintings did not have to look like something else; the public did not have to like them; art critics did not have to understand them. But they had to be shown. Gallery 291 was sometimes called the largest small room in the world. It was a small attic loft at the top of a Fifth Avenue brownstone house. The artists who exhibited there had great talent, and eventually they all became famous.

In May of 1916 Alfred Stieglitz hung Georgia O'Keeffe's drawings on the walls of 291 along with paintings by two other artists. He thought the drawings were exciting and fresh because they were abstract; that is, they were not a drawing of some other object. Abstract art is art work that portrays shapes, lines, or colors without any attempt to represent some "real" object, like a tree, a landscape, or a portrait of a person. At that time abstract art had rarely been seen in the United States. Years later, after World War II, it became a very popular form of expression by American artists.

By now Georgia O'Keeffe had returned to New York to finish her art studies at Columbia University. When she heard about the exhibit, she went straight downtown to 291 to demand that the drawings be taken down. She had been to the gallery only once before, years earlier when she was a student at the Art Students League. She took the elevator up to the loft and faced Alfred Stieglitz, a spare, slight man, twenty-three years older than she was. Georgia explained that she had sent the drawings to a close friend for her private viewing and did not intend to show them to anyone else. Would he please take the drawings down?

Alfred Stieglitz quietly persuaded her that the work had great merit. The drawings were exciting emotional expressions; they should be seen by others. She relented and returned uptown to Columbia. That summer after she had left New York, Stieglitz photographed the drawings and sent the photographs to her, which pleased her very much.

Georgia O'Keeffe now became head of the art department at West Texas Normal College, a school that trained teachers. The teaching job gave her free time to paint on her own. She continued to draw the abstract sketches, but she also did watercolors inspired by the vast, flat landscape. Sometimes she got up before sunrise to walk to the station and see the train racing out of the dawn. Many times she walked miles away from the tiny town. A friendship had developed between Stieglitz and O'Keeffe, and she mailed him some of the drawings and watercolors she did.

In May of 1917 he hung these drawings in her first one-man show at 291. He wrote to her that the building was being torn down and that hers was to be the final exhibit. At the end of the school year, she traveled to

New York to see the gallery one last time, only to find that Stieglitz had already closed the gallery and taken down her drawings. Nevertheless, he rehung the show for her and photographed her with the drawings. This was the first of his many famous photographs of her.

After another year of teaching school in Texas, Georgia returned to New York for the summer. Stieglitz felt that she should give up her teaching career and concentrate full-time on art. He was able to offer financial support to the small group of artists whom he exhibited in his gallery, and he offered to support Georgia O'Keeffe.

She wanted to accept, but she hesitated. She knew that she could teach art. But what about painting full-time? What if no one else liked the paintings? What if Stieglitz could not sell anything? She understood that a full-time career of painting was a risk, like "walking on a knife edge," she later said. But it was a great opportunity, and she accepted.

Georgia O'Keeffe, now thirty-one years old, settled into a studio in New York, where she spent the winters painting. In the spring she usually went with Alfred Stieglitz to Lake George, where his family had a large estate. As one might expect, the wooded lake scenery began to appear in her art. Often the paintings were dark and somber, with brooding clouds or black crows flying over the lake. Sometimes she did studies of the rippling water that looked like her abstract works.

She continued to work on her abstract studies. She now progressed from charcoal drawings to oils. Some of these oil paintings, with titles like *Blue and Green Music,* display abstract rhythmic patterns. Others look like the pastel heart of an iris, or some exotic jungle flower. Still others show strong slashes of vibrant orange. The oils were a bolder way to portray her inner visions. This was a maturing process for her art, wholly her own. Though some European artists now began to paint in the abstract style, she was not affected by them. Throughout her life, she kept her vow to paint totally for herself, and her art remained her own expression.

All of this hard work resulted in a large "one-man" show in 1923. One hundred of her drawings and oil paintings were shown at Anderson Galleries during Janu-

Georgia O'Keeffe, Blue and Green Music, *1919.*

ary and February. At first she seemed shy about exposing so much of her work, when there already were so many exhibitions. "It seems ridiculous to add to the mess," she wrote in the catalog. But she had to admit she wanted to see her things hanging on a wall. And she wanted others to see them and comment on them.

The art critics recognized that she painted from her own ideas and visions. They also thought that her abstract works advanced the cause of modern or abstract art in the United States. Just as impressionism had been resisted in Paris fifty years before, modern art was now resisted in the United States.

In addition to concentrating on her painting every day, Georgia posed for Alfred to photograph her. These photographs were not simply pictures of Georgia O'Keeffe; they were artistic works in themselves. Stieglitz was a pioneer in believing that a photograph was as artistic as a painting. He is considered the founder of photography as an art form.

From the time he first knew Georgia O'Keeffe until he stopped photographing, Stieglitz took more than five hundred pictures of her. This extensive portrait collection has been called the greatest love poem since the *Song of Solomon* in the Bible.

In 1924 he arranged an exhibit of his photographs to hang with her paintings at the Anderson Galleries. Here the work of the famous photographer was joined with the work of the modern painter. Later that year they joined their lives as well and were married.

After their marriage, someone called Georgia O'Keeffe Mrs. Stieglitz. "Miss O'Keeffe," she corrected. She always used her own family name. Because of her refusal to take the name of her husband and because of her modern painting, Georgia O'Keeffe became a model of the "liberated" woman. At this time, only four years after women had gained the right to vote, an independent, modern woman was admired very much.

The couple lived on the thirty-ninth floor of the Shelton Hotel. From their high window, Georgia looked out on the East River and the tall buildings. The city excited her, and she painted bold, geometric paintings of soaring skyscrapers. Sometimes they were bathed in shimmering light, like *Shelton Hotel with Sun Spots.* A night scene of the Radiator Building had the name *Alfred Stieglitz* glowing in neon letters, a tribute to her husband.

During the 1920s there were many new skyscrapers

A photograph of Georgia O'Keeffe by Alfred Stieglitz, taken in 1918.

soaring upward in New York. They inspired another subject for Georgia O'Keeffe's art. Just as the buildings were growing to enormous size around her, she decided to blow flowers up to huge proportions. She took one single blossom and filled the entire canvas with it. Sometimes she painted only a part of one single flower. The flowers were painted as accurately as a close-up photograph. But the paintings had more life and vibrancy than a photograph.

The large flower paintings were startling, and many times she was asked about their meaning. She said that if she painted flowers in normal proportions, just as everyone else had, no one would really look at them. But if she took a single blossom and enlarged it to an enormous size, then everyone, even busy New Yorkers, would take the time to look at them. They would really see the flower exactly as it was. Indeed, the flowers were noticed, and Georgia O'Keeffe became famous for these paintings.

It was now, in the summer of 1929, that she made that first trip to Mabel Dodge's art colony in Taos, that would ever after focus her life and her art on the New Mexico desert. She still spent the winter in New York, but she returned each summer to the desert. Because she preferred to work alone, she abandoned the art colony in Taos. By herself, she went to Abiquiu, a small village north of Taos in the Chama River Valley.

Someone had told Georgia that the most beautiful spot in the United States was Ghost Ranch, New Mexico, and she went there and rented a house.

Ghost Ranch was so arid that nothing but sage brush would grow there. But Georgia O'Keeffe loved the badlands that rolled away from her door to barren cliffs and mountains. The reds, purples, and copper green of the desert were as bright as the pigments on her palette. She painted the hills in a bright, pure way. Not everyone thought the hill paintings were as pretty as the flower ones, but she claimed that the hills touched her heart as much as the flowers. As she did in the flower paintings, she had a way of leaving out details and getting right at the heart of the landscape.

After she returned to her husband in New York for the winter, she sometimes painted the bones that she had collected on her desert walks. The bone paintings began to appear in her yearly exhibits. In one painting, a cow's skull is presented like an emblem on a red, white, and dark blue banner. The horns of the skull and the banner form a cross. A later painting called *Summer Days* shows a deer skull with a small cluster of flowers floating over the red mountains and blue sky of New Mexico. The skulls were painted realistically, with great skill, much as the flowers had been.

When the skull paintings first appeared, some critics regarded them as strange, depressing symbols of death. One writer said that she returned from the West with gruesome trophies. But as the bone paintings appeared year after year during the 1930s, people began to regard them differently. The bones were seen as part of a whole cycle of life. Sometimes they were compared to wild-flowers, because they were whitened by the wind and sun. The wear and tear of nature was not frightening to Georgia O'Keeffe. She said that she found the bones "more living than the animals walking around—hair, eyes, and all with their tails switching. The bones seem to cut sharply to the center of something that is keenly alive on the desert."

After painting skulls, she concentrated on pelvis bones. The holes in the pelvis bones especially fasci-nated her. She painted them floating like exotic creatures against vibrant blue skies. Sometimes the background appeared as bright red or orange, instead of bright blue. She painted more than fifteen of these pelvises for an

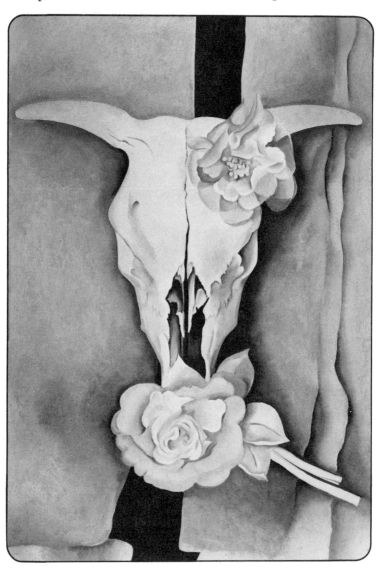

Georgia O'Keeffe, Cow's Skull with Calico Roses, *1931.*

exhibition and enjoyed seeing them all hanging together.

Her fame as an artist had spread far beyond the circle of people interested in modern art in New York. In 1938 O'Keeffe was awarded an honorary degree, a Doctor of Fine Arts, from William and Mary College in Williamsburg. In 1939 she was chosen one of twelve most outstanding women of the past fifty years by the New York World's Fair Tomorrow Committee.

In 1942 the University of Wisconsin awarded her an honorary Doctor of Literature degree, noting that her paintings hung in the Metropolitan Museum, the Museum of Modern Art, and the Whitney Museum—all famous New York museums.

Recognition in the art world spread beyond New York. The Chicago Art Institute held her first full-scale retrospective exhibit in 1943. A retrospective is an exhibition that contains art works that span an artist's entire career. She selected the paintings, crated them, and went to Chicago for the exhibit. Seeing a sample of everything she had ever painted was like seeing her biography written on the wall: the paintings were her life.

During the early 1940s, she returned to the Ghost Ranch adobe house to paint each summer. She loved the isolation of the ranch, where days might go by without someone passing on the road. But since there was no water, all her food had to be brought in. She was getting tired of canned food. She ate simply, but she liked fresh fruits and vegetables. In Abiquiu in the Chama River Valley she could have a garden.

She had seen in Abiquiu an old tumble down house with a marvelous view, and she wanted to buy it. Since it had been promised to a church, the owners did not want to sell it. Finally, after asking and negotiating for ten years, she bought the crumbling structure in 1945.

She found some women in the village who knew how to repair adobe, and she hired them to rebuild a cluster of rooms around a patio. Large windows provided a magnificent view of the valley. Even when she could not paint outdoors, the mesas and hills across the river were visible. Every room in the house had an open fireplace, where fragrant piñon logs burned in cool weather. Now, in addition to the house at Ghost Ranch, she had a house in the village with a garden. Eventually the garden at Abiquiu yielded everything from rutabagas to endive. All of her bread was homemade from wheat ground at her house.

During the next three years, Georgia O'Keeffe could spend little time in New Mexico. Her husband died in New York on July 13, 1946, at the age of eighty-two. After nearly a half-century of owning an art gallery in New York City, Stieglitz had built up an extensive collection of modern art. He owned paintings by European artists Matisse, Rodin, and Picasso, who had been exhibited in the early years of his gallery. He also had many works by American artists, for he felt strongly that modern art must come from the United States as well as Europe. Besides paintings by Georgia O'Keeffe, there were works by John Marin, Marsten Hartley, Arthur Dove, and Charles Demuth. And his collection contained his famous photographs. It was his wish that this large collection be donated to museums, so that the art could be shared with the people of the United States.

The task of dividing the collection and deciding where to send the paintings fell to Georgia O'Keeffe. She worked at this with the same concentration and effort she put into her art. She spent brief periods of the summers in New Mexico, but she had little time for painting. From 1946 to 1949 she worked long hours each day going over the extensive Stieglitz collection.

Finally, in the summer of 1949 the enormous task of sorting, cataloging, and distributing the paintings and photographs to museums was completed, and Georgia settled permanently in New Mexico. During the cold months she lived in the comfortable adobe house in Abiquiu. Looking out of the big windows, she could see the winter-stripped cottonwood trees in the valley. She painted the trees to look like ghosts with tentacles looming out of the winter mists.

One area of her house particularly fascinated her— a single door set in the long, straight patio wall. She claimed that she bought the house because she was attracted to the patio door. She felt she had to paint the door in the massive wall over and over. "I never quite get it. It's a curse the way I feel I must go on with that door," she said in an interview with Katharine Kuh.

As she did in her other series paintings, in the early works she painted a realistic view of the opening in the wall. Then, as the subject was repeated, the paintings became abstract, bold designs inspired by the same wall. An early painting shows the wall brilliantly lit in the sun; the opening in the thick adobe is heavily shadowed. A later, much larger painting done in 1960 is a sharp-edged pink rectangle set in a seven-foot-long expanse of white. Smaller pink rectangles at the base of the painting represent tiles around the door.

After a few years of the rhythm of living at Ghost Ranch in the summer and moving to Abiquiu for the winter, O'Keeffe was ready to travel. As a student, and later during her career, she never had the urge to travel to Europe to see the work of the masters. Other artists never influenced her, neither old masters nor modern artists. When she chose to travel, in her mid-sixties, she was most interested in seeing the countries and the people. In 1953 she took her first trip to Europe. She liked the bullfights in Spain and returned the following year. In 1959 she traveled around the world, a trip that lasted three months, and she discovered that she liked the Orient better than Europe. The next year she went back to Japan and Southeast Asia.

Foreign countries were not the only thing that attracted her. In 1961, when she was seventy-three years old, she made her first raft trip down the rapids of the Colorado River. She found the trip so exciting that she repeated the adventure several times.

The experience of flying in airplanes on these long trips influenced Georgia O'Keeffe's painting. She painted rivers curving and cutting across the countryside, the way she saw them from the plane. The painting could have been one of her earlier abstract patterns. But she said that was exactly what the river looked like; there was nothing abstract about it.

In the early 1960s she began to paint studies of clouds. The clouds appear as they would from an airplane. The first paintings in the series are of realistic, fluffy clouds. Then the size of the paintings increased and the clouds became more individually shaped and precisely defined, like white rectangular stepping stones.

The final work of the series, *Sky above Clouds IV,* is twenty-four feet wide, the largest canvas Georgia O'Keeffe ever painted. She spent the entire summer of 1965 working on the painting in her double garage studio at Ghost Ranch. The clouds in the painting stretch out to the horizon, where they disappear over the curve of the earth. The horizon, vastly far away, is rosy colored like the dawn. The sky is a band of pale blue at the top of the painting.

This painting is considered her masterpiece. People lucky enough to have seen it say that they felt as though they were looking out at the endless sky from a high-flying airplane. The painting does not look exactly like the sky from an airplane, but Georgia O'Keeffe has captured the way it feels to look out of an airplane at the infinity of space.

All of these paintings continued to bring O'Keeffe recognition and honors during the 1950s and 1960s. In 1963 she was elected to the American Academy of Arts and Letters. In 1966, the American Academy of Arts and Sciences elected her to membership, and the National Institute of Arts and Letters awarded her their Gold Medal for Painting.

Many magazine articles have been written about her. Writers for art and fashion magazines are eager to visit her adobe home in Abiquiu to interview and photograph her. Throughout her career, articles about her paintings have appeared in art magazines. She is a favorite subject in fashion magazines because of her striking appearance and her choice to live alone on the desert.

Like her paintings, her appearance also seems to be pared down to only those characteristics that reflect her inner self. In the 1950s, as her hair turned gray, she wore it pulled straight back to reveal all of the contours of her face. More recent photographs show her hairstyle unchanged. When she is photographed, she usually faces the camera directly, looking straight into the lens.

When interviewers ask her about her art, she says little. "Painting is my language," she says. "It is the way I speak." Modern American art is enriched by this language of timeless beauty and unique vision in the paintings of Georgia O'Keeffe.

Louise Nevelson creates monumental assemblages of wood and other materials.

An Empire in Wood

LOUISE NEVELSON

In 1941 sculptor Louise Nevelson had scarcely enough money for rent and art supplies. The basement of her house on Twenty-first Street in New York was filled with modern sculptures that had not sold. For the past ten years, while studying art and beginning her career as a sculptor, she had lived on money from her family and on the sale of her jewels. Now all the jewels were gone. It seemed that her dreams of a successful artistic career were gone too.

Before giving up, though, she decided to try a bold idea. She would call on the best dealer in New York and simply ask him to arrange an exhibit that would sell her work. She went to Karl Nierendorf, who owned a gallery on East Fifty-seventh Street. Calmly, she told him that she wanted to exhibit in his gallery.

Nierendorf was taken aback by her bold approach, but he agreed to look at her work. That evening he went to her studio and examined the low, modern figures made of clay and wood. The quality impressed him, and to her surprise he agreed to exhibit the figures within a month.

A few weeks later her sculptures were placed in Nierendorf's gallery, and at age forty-two, Louise Nevelson finally had her first one-man exhibit. Most important of all, Karl Nierendorf offered her financial support that allowed her to continue her art work without supporting herself in some other way.

It was a fine beginning, but her association with the Nierendorf Gallery did not last forever, and later Louise Nevelson would find herself in poverty again. Many times during her life, Louise Nevelson has lived through defeats that would have ended the artistic career of anyone less strong than she is. But she has always recovered. Her art has always grown and expanded in spite of many personal setbacks. Today she is internationally famous for her enormous sculptures in black wood.

She was born in Kiev, Russia, in 1899. Her parents, Mina and Isaac Berliawsky, did not record the exact date of her birth, but she celebrates her birthday on September twenty-third. When Louise was two years old, her father, a building contractor and lumber merchant, decided to improve his fortunes in the United States. He emigrated to Rockland, Maine, but left the rest of the family behind in Kiev until he could establish a home for them. Louise missed her father so much that she stopped talking for six months.

Finally, after two years of hard work, Mr. Berliawsky sent for his family. Louise's earliest memory is of an event that occurred on the voyage from Russia to the United States. At a stop in Liverpool, England, Louise visited a candy store on the dock with her mother, brother, and sister. The shop had stacks of shining glass jars filled with purple, green, and red candies, glowing like amethysts, emeralds, and rubies. Even at four years old, she responded to the sight like an artist; the colors and the arrangement of the jars are what she remembers, not the taste of the candy.

The Berliawsky children arrived in Maine wearing Persian lamb coats and speaking only Russian. Louise felt different from the American children who wore woolen coats and who played games she did not understand. But by the time Louise started school she could speak English quite well, and she had learned some of the games. As their father's business prospered, the Berliawsky family settled into the New England pattern of life. But Louise still felt set apart from the other children. She always had one close friend, but her interests were not shared by most of the other children her age.

After school she had little time to play, since she was busy with lessons or practicing. She studied painting, piano, and voice. Later, to learn how to move freely and easily, she studied dance.

One thing Louise always enjoyed was moving the furniture around. She loved to try different arrangements in the rooms. Another thing she liked was going to her father's lumber yard and picking up scraps of wood. Sometimes she changed the shape of a piece by carving it; sometimes she fit smaller pieces together to build a larger piece. Later, as an adult, she built her sculptures by the same process of picking up wood scraps and then fitting them together to form a larger piece.

In school, art was the only subject that interested her. She was a slow reader and never read one word more than the required assignments. In second grade the teacher showed the students a sunflower and then asked them to go home and draw the flower from memory. What Louise remembered best was the huge round center, and she drew a big circle that nearly covered the paper. The petals were tiny spikes that radiated from the center like the sun. The following day the teacher said that Louise's sunflower was the most original, and it was the only drawing pinned on the wall.

Art continued to be her favorite subject in high school. Her teacher there was a graduate of Pratt Art Institute in Brooklyn, New York, and Louise considered studying art at Pratt.

During her senior year in high school, she met Charles Nevelson, who was already working in his family's shipping business. Louise, who was eighteen years old, had never dated before. They became engaged almost immediately. They were married two years later, in 1920, and moved to New York City.

As the wife of a young, prosperous New York businessman, Louise was invited to play games like Mah-Jongg and to attend afternoon tea parties. But games and idle chatter did not interest her. For her, moving to New York meant the opportunity to study art and music in a way she had only dreamed about in Rockland. She studied voice with Estelle Liebling, a Metropolitan Opera coach. She took private painting lessons and, looking for other ways to express herself, studied drama.

In 1922 their son Mike was born. Caring for a tiny baby took more time and energy, but since the Nevelsons had servants to clean the house and cook the meals, Louise was able to continue her studies. In 1928 she enrolled in the Art Students League. By now her interest in art dominated her interest in voice and drama. She loved her painting classes so much that it was difficult to put down her brushes and be home for dinner at seven-thirty when her husband expected her. She felt an increasing conflict between being a wife and mother and being an artist. Eventually she decided that she had to make a choice; she could no longer be both.

Either choice was painful and demanded a price from her. But she wanted to be an artist, and she felt that she had enough talent and courage to choose art over the comforts of family life. In 1931, after eleven years of marriage, she separated from her husband, asking for no support or alimony. All that she had left from the marriage were some jewels, and over the following years she sold them one by one to help support herself.

She took Mike to stay with her parents in Maine, and she went to Munich to study art with Hans Hofmann, an outstanding teacher of modern painting. She went daily to drawing classes, where she learned a new technique called cubism. Modern painters in Paris, particularly Picasso, had invented this new style of painting. Cubist painters divide objects into simple geometric shapes and paint these shapes flat against the canvas. Later, when she became a sculptor, Louise Nevelson created her first works in the cubist style.

Though there were only twelve students in Louise Nevelson's drawing class, she saw Hans Hofmann only about once a week. He had problems of his own. During the early 1930s the Nazi party was pushing its way to power in Germany. The Nazis were hostile to many things, including Jews and modern art. Since Hans Hofmann was both Jewish and a modern artist, he eventually closed the art school and went to the United States.

She was disappointed at his departure, but she stayed on in Munich. In the evenings she would go to the cafés with other art students, American writers, and movie makers. One night Louise was asked to sing some spirituals. She had a beautiful voice, and a scenarist for the movies heard her and invited her to be in a movie in Vienna. However, she soon became bored with acting; being a painter, she was most interested in the movie sets and lights. After a few minor roles in films whose names she cannot recall, she left Vienna and movie making.

She traveled through Italy and finally decided to go to Paris to study paintings of the old masters. She went to the Louvre, as Mary Cassatt had done fifty years earlier. She also went to an exhibit of African art. This exhibit was especially interesting to her, because the bold, simple shapes of African masks had originally inspired Picasso to paint in the cubist style.

Being alone in Paris gave her time to think about her accomplishments as an artist. She felt discouraged, because she had not reached her goals. But then, she was not even certain what the goals were. She felt guilty for leaving her old life; she was doubtful about creating a new one. She became very depressed, and there seemed to be nothing to do but go home.

Louise returned to New York and again entered classes at the Art Students League. She now studied sculpture, as well as drawing and painting. Restless again, after nine months she decided to return to Paris. She sold some jewels to buy a ticket on the liner *France*.

After she had been studying in Paris for only a few weeks, she realized that French art rested on the greatness of the past and that the future of art was in New York. So Louise Nevelson made the reverse journey of Mary Cassatt. In 1873, Mary Cassatt had settled in Paris because the art world was centered there. By 1932, Louise Nevelson realized that the center of the art world had shifted to the United States, and she returned to New York. It has been her home ever since. Louise enrolled once more at the Art Students League. Hans Hofmann, after leaving Germany, was now teaching there, and she arranged to be in his classes.

Some of the line drawings of the human figure from

Louise Nevelson's life class survive today. The proportions of the figures are not accurate. Often the head or legs are missing. The figures suggest mass and weight, and they look like the drawings of a sculptor, rather than those of a painter who paints on a flat surface. She was already interested in portraying figures in three dimensions.

During 1933 she became an apprentice to Diego Rivera, who was painting large murals for Rockefeller Center and other public buildings in New York. He painted scenes of people working in factories and on farms for these enormous wall paintings, and he needed apprentices to help him, since the murals were so large. Louise Nevelson and other apprentices took his small sketches, drew them on the wall on a very large scale in exactly the same proportion as the small drawings, and then painted over the drawing to create the mural. She was learning techniques of painting in this work, but it was not very satisfying, because it was not her own art and did not express her own ideas.

But Diego Rivera introduced Nevelson to another important influence on her own art—pre-Columbian art, the primitive art of the Central American Indians. The sculpture, architecture, and masks of these Indians made a real impression on her, just as cubism and African art had impressed her in Paris. She began to sculpt figures which show the influences of both primitive art and cubism. Carved from wood or made from clay, the head of the figure might be a cube with a face carved in simple, straight planes like an Indian mask. The body, arms, and legs were simply rectangles set at right angles to each other. They looked both very old and very modern.

Nevelson entered some of these cubist figures in group exhibits in the mid-1930s, and she received some mention in the reviews of these exhibits. Along with four other young artists, she was invited to exhibit again at one of the galleries. A review of this exhibit singled her work out as the most interesting. This was needed encouragement at a time when she was working alone, without gaining much recognition or even selling her art. She had continued to sell jewels to pay for art materials, food, and rent.

In 1933, she left the Art Students League and her formal art studies. Restlessly, she moved from one room to another. She would create enough sculpture to fill one studio; then she would move on to the next. There are only a few pieces of her work that survive from this period. She did not seem to care if things were lost or destroyed. Even though she was no longer a student, she was searching and finding herself as an artist.

Toward the end of the 1930s her jewels were nearly all sold. She was very poor, as were many Americans during the depression of the 1930s. The Works Progress Administration (WPA), created by President Roosevelt in 1935 to give work to unemployed people, offered jobs for writers and artists. Under this program, Nevelson taught sculpture at the Educational Alliance School of Art in Lower Manhattan.

Unfortunately, the WPA ended in 1938, and she lost her teaching job. By 1941, with her jewels all gone and without another source of income, she was in a desperate situation. It was then that she went to Karl Nierendorf and formed the association with the Nierendorf Gallery that led to her first one-man show and to improved financial security.

After this show, she began a new phase of her art. She began to create her sculptures using a new technique: Instead of carving wood or molding clay into squared, cubist forms, she picked up pieces of wood, metal, or even fabric and nailed or glued the scraps and pieces together to form larger figures. This technique of putting together scraps to make a larger piece is called assemblage. Nevelson has used this technique to create her sculpture ever since. The style of the finished sculpture has changed, and she has sometimes changed the materials she works with, but the process of building up the sculpture from smaller pieces has remained the same.

Her third one-man show at the Nierendorf Gallery, in 1943, consisted entirely of assembled wood and metal sculptures. Instead of just setting the figures around the gallery to be viewed one by one, she grouped them all together, creating a fantasy world. She named it *The Circus—The Clown Is the Center of the World.* The walls of the gallery were hung with circus posters. Then she arranged the sculptures into three groups: *The Menagerie,* whimsical animals; *The Clowns,* cubist human figures; and *The World Outside,* stacked figures suggesting the audience. Some of the figures moved, and one cried with tears made of broken bits of mirror.

The cubist clowns and performers in the circus represented a strange new way to create and exhibit sculpture. Even in New York in the 1940s, when painters and sculptors were experimenting with many styles, the public and even art critics did not always accept the newest ideas. Worried about the reaction to her assembled circus, Nevelson also exhibited a series of her line drawings at the same time.

She should not have worried. The reviews of *The Circus* were favorable. However, none of the pieces sold. Disappointed, Nevelson had the pieces trucked back to her Tenth Street studio. The storage area was already crowded, so she dismantled the pieces. She burned the parts she could not use again and saved the other scraps for future pieces.

In 1943 Nevelson's father died, and she inherited some money from his estate. She used it to buy a house on Thirtieth Street. The house was not grand, but it suited her. A stone ledge in the garden served as her workbench, where she began to assemble wooden sculptures called "landscapes." Small enough to fit on a table top or a pedestal, the landscapes were often composed of chair legs, carvings that once trimmed Victorian houses, or smooth doughnut shapes. They are not landscapes in the sense of paintings of fields or forests. The wooden pieces are arranged to suggest buildings or structures in a city. One piece with two tiny carved lions looks like the entrance to some fairy-tale ancient city.

In her 1944 show, Nevelson exhibited these landscapes, as well as oil paintings of several of her friends. With the financial security of Nierendorf Gallery, where she had yearly exhibits during most of the 1940s, she enjoyed the freedom of working on her own sculpture and painting without worries about money.

Her exhibit for 1948 was supposed to be arranged with Karl Nierendorf after he returned from a collecting trip in Germany. The night before her appointment, a friend telephoned to tell her that Nierendorf had died. She simply could not believe it and would not believe it until she read it in the newspaper the following morning.

Nierendorf's death was a severe blow for her. Not only was her financial protection gone, but so was his belief in her as a sculptor, which had been very encouraging. She did not have the heart to try to make another gallery association. She found it nearly impossible to work. Then, to compound things, she became ill and had to have surgery to remove a tumor.

Once again she plunged into despair, as she had when she was alone in Paris and again as she had just before she approached Nierendorf in 1941. Concerned about her health, her friends encouraged her to travel, and she went to Europe with her sister Anita.

On her return, still weakened physically, she found that she could no longer work with heavy pieces of wood, and she began to work with clay. Again she used the technique of assemblage. Instead of molding and building up a figure as most sculptors do, she flattened the clay and cut out forms. The process was like rolling and cutting out thick cookies. She assembled these flat clay pieces on a pole to form a cubist figure. She named the finished forms *Game Figures.*

This period of work in clay was a kind of holding period in her development as a sculptor. She believes that she works in cycles. One cycle of her work had stopped, and the next had not begun.

Nevelson had retained her interest in pre-Columbian art ever since learning about it from Diego Rivera, and when the Museum of Natural History exhibited some pre-Columbian monuments called steles, she eagerly went to see them. Made by the Indians of Mexico, steles are stone pillars with carved, inscribed surfaces. Geometric images and elaborate designs encrust the entire surface. Later, richly decorated columns resembling the steles appeared in Nevelson's own work.

Soon Nevelson again began to work in wood. Another creative cycle was beginning, and her art was again growing. She chose large natural slabs of wood, set them upright on a base, and attached spikes to the edge of the large piece. One called *Indian Chief* looks like the profile of an Indian wearing a feather war bonnet. She painted the entire piece dull black. From this time on, she unified all of the wooden scraps of her sculpture by painting them a single color, usually dull black.

By 1955 she seemed again ready to exhibit her work. Colette Roberts, director of Grand Central Moderns Gallery, arranged for an exhibit that contained some of the clay figures, the wooden "landscapes," and the black wooden sculptures. These were all individual pieces and did not relate to each other. In her exhibit the following year, she returned to the idea of creating many pieces with a common theme and arranging them together, as she had in *The Circus.* In the new exhibit, named *Royal Voyage,* tall figures she called kings and queens looked out over the gallery as though it were some ancient sea. Placed before them on the floor were chunky wooden forms representing royal gifts.

Nevelson frequently used this idea of relating all of the sculptures in an exhibit to a common theme, arranging them in the gallery to create a total environment or fantasy world. Her most ambitious work of this type was *Moon Garden Plus One,* exhibited in 1958. This fantasy land grew out of the scraps of wood that Nevelson kept in bins in her Thirtieth Street house. She collected sweepings from lumber yards and furniture factories. She scoured junk shops and the streets of New York for castoffs. She accumulated crates and planks. She painted everything black. Then, just as a painter dips into different colored paints, she picked up her different sizes and shapes of wood and glued or nailed them to the flat wooden slabs.

Almost anything became art in her hands. One of the pieces in *Moon Garden Plus One* was inspired by a carton of liquor she received for Christmas. She set the carton on its side and observed that with its individual compartments for bottles, it could be a sculpture. She began to stack wooden crates on their side with the open end facing front. The insides of the crates were filled with wooden scraps, glued to the surface like jigsaw pieces that did not match. She stacked the crates on top of each other, higher and higher until they became an entire wall. Called *Sky Cathedral,* this was the first of her many walls, sculptures for which she is now famous.

Louise Nevelson, Sky Cathedral, *1958. Collection, The Museum of Modern Art, New York.*

When Nevelson arrived at the gallery with all of the separate pieces of sculpture for *Moon Garden Plus One,* she arranged them in the gallery just as carefully as she chose the small scraps for her sculptures. She wanted visitors to the gallery to feel that they had stepped into an eerie moon garden, an unearthly place. She and her assistant, Teddy Hazeltine, blackened out the windows with paper and placed some of the sculptures in front of them. It would be like entering a movie theatre from the sunlight; only gradually would the visitor make out the dim inhabitants of the garden. A blue light was used to emphasize the interplay of forms and shadows. The shadows of Nevelson's black sculptures are as important as the wood forms themselves. Many times the wooden scraps dissolve into shadow. The whole structure takes on a magic, ghostly quality, like a building in a dream.

Art critics enthusiastically praised *Moon Garden Plus One.* One writer said that the *Sky Cathedral* wall sculpture in this exhibit was the sum of every artistic idea she had ever used. After the exhibit was dismantled, *Sky Cathedral* was donated to the Museum of Modern Art. Unfortunately none of the other large pieces sold.

With the success of *Moon Garden Plus One,* Nevelson became a celebrity in the art world. Museum directors came to see her work. French artists expressed interest in her sculpture, and she started to exhibit with a Paris dealer named Daniel Cordier. Since Grand Central Moderns Gallery could not afford to support her and the large cost of working with enormous sculpture, she signed a contract with Martha Jackson Gallery. She was guaranteed yearly sales, or the gallery itself would purchase her work to provide a salary for her. After working thirty years as an artist, she was at last able to support herself comfortably on her art. She was fifty-eight years old.

Her first exhibit at Martha Jackson was *Sky Columns,* in 1959. Set against walls that she had painted black, the sculptures were tall, narrow forms like the Mexican steles.

That same year Nevelson was invited to participate in an exhibit of sixteen American artists at the Museum of Modern Art. It was her first opportunity to show her work in a major museum, and she wanted to do something new. She rented work space in a building and painted the walls entirely white. She began to paint the scraps she worked with white, since she had decided she did not want color contrasts. Finally she assembled the white pieces into fantasy structures. The result was called *Dawn's Wedding Feast.*

No one was allowed to see the finished pieces. She wanted absolute secrecy about the white forms. Late in the afternoon, just before the exhibit was to open, she had the pieces trucked to the museum. She and Teddy Hazeltine and only two helpers from the museum staff installed the entire show. For Nevelson the installation was the dessert of *Dawn's Wedding Feast.* The meal had been prepared in the studio.

Although the white forms are constructed exactly like the black pieces, the appearance of the white is very different. The small pieces do not disappear into shadow; the shape and contour of each fragment stand out. Instead of walking in a ghostly garden, the viewers travel a sunlit street lined with old-fashioned white houses.

At the end of the exhibit Nevelson hoped that some museum would buy the entire *Dawn's Wedding Feast.* She wanted one of her complete environments to be saved. But no collector or museum bought it. A few pieces sold separately; a few have been reassembled into smaller exhibit pieces. But the members and guests of *Dawn's Wedding Feast* are scattered forever.

In 1959 Nevelson bought a larger house at 29 Spring Street, where she still lives. The house had been a sanitarium and had marble staircases and an iron grill double door. Sometimes the door is painted in the color that Nevelson is currently working in.

After she moved to the new house she painted one wall gold. She also painted the wooden scraps gold, and assembled them into *Royal Tides,* her 1961 exhibit at Martha Jackson Gallery. Besides working in a new color, she started to stack boxes of the same shape and size for the wall sculptures. Previously she had used a mixture of orange, apple, and tomato packing crates in the same wall. Now she created a grid structure with crates of the same size. The regular grid added unity. The gold color seemed to give weight to the pieces. They actually seemed made of gold, rather than wood sprayed with gold paint. Art critics and reviewers in general did not like the gold as much as the black or white. Nevelson created gold sculptures throughout the 1960s, but black has remained the basic color of her work.

By now Nevelson had a worldwide reputation. In 1962 she was invited to represent the United States at the Venice Biennale. Held every two years in Italy, the Biennale is the World's Fair of art. Each country sends art works by its best known artists. Since the paintings and sculptures are works that the artists have recently completed, the Biennale exhibits represent the most modern art created in the world.

In the United States Pavillion, Nevelson had one room painted white, another gold, and another black. She arranged to have Cordier, her Paris dealer, send sculptures to Venice. Then she arranged white, gold, and black walls in rooms of the same color. Using all three colors side by side, she gave visitors the opportunity to experience all three environments. Nevelson's work was the sensation of the Biennale. Afterwards, the pieces were dismantled and never again arranged in this way.

The Biennale led to another invitation for Nevelson: Sidney Janis offered to be her art dealer. At the time the Sidney Janis Gallery represented a group of the most famous painters in New York. Nevelson was the first woman invited to exhibit there and the first American sculptor. The invitation was a triumph for her.

She assembled three massive, beautiful walls for her first exhibit. Again one was white, one black, and the other gold. But it was the first time she had worked on three colors at once. The festive opening was on New

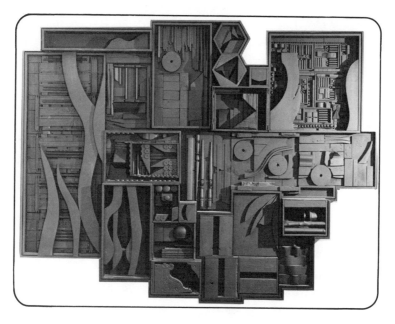

Louise Nevelson, Night Zag Wall, *1973-75.*

Year's Eve of 1963. Since the New York newspapers were on strike, the exhibit was not well publicized or reviewed. The lack of attention seemed to be an omen of the difficulties that followed. Only one small piece of sculpture sold. The contract with Sidney Janis did not guarantee her a salary. Since her work did not sell, Nevelson was in debt to him for the money she had needed to create and install the three walls.

She sold her Spring Street house, but she was able to continue living in the house by renting it from the new owner. The money from the sale paid for an attorney who figured out a legal way that she could break the contract with Sidney Janis Gallery. She was able to break the contract, but Sidney Janis kept the three massive walls as collateral until she could raise the money to buy them back. Most of her other work was owned by her previous dealers, Martha Jackson, and Daniel Cordier in Paris. Depressed and discouraged, at sixty-three years old she had a worldwide reputation, but she owned almost none of her work and she was deeply in debt. She seemed unable to go on creating the wooden sculpture.

Then an opportunity for travel and for a new area of work appeared when she needed to escape from New York and she needed to earn money. She was invited to go to the Tamarind Lithography Workshop in Los Angeles. Lithographs are prints made by inking the design on a stone. They are different from engravings, which use metal plates. The Tamarind Lithography Workshop invites famous artists, like Nevelson, to come and make a series of prints. This enables people who could never afford to buy one of Nevelson's wood sculptures to buy one of her prints. Original prints are numbered and signed individually by the artist. After six weeks in Los Angeles she had produced more sets of prints than any other artist in the history of the Tamarind Lithography Workshop.

When she got back to New York, she was refreshed and ready to return to work on wood sculpture. Again using black scraps of wood, she created a curved wall called *Homage 6,000,000.* It was eighteen feet wide and nine feet high. Sometimes she tried new shapes for the walls by stacking the boxes into triangles. She glued mirrors into the back of the boxes. The mirrors reflected the wooden fragments and appeared to add depth to the boxes. Viewers who peer closely at these walls are also reflected in the mirrors and become part of the sculpture itself. Sometimes Nevelson covered the front of the boxes with plexiglass. This too can reflect, like the windows of a lighted room at night. Sometimes she cut the scale of her work down to a size small enough to be hung on a wall. *Diminishing Reflections* is made up of miniature boxes only two inches square filled with chess pawns, checkers, and tiny scraps. Often she ordered dozens of boxes of Lincoln Logs and blocks from Macy's toy department.

After her difficulties with Sidney Janis, Nevelson became associated with Pace Gallery, where she has yearly exhibitions. By 1966 her work was selling to both museums and private collectors. She no longer felt financially insecure, and she was able to buy back the Spring Street house. Now, one might think, she could relax and perhaps take time to enjoy her home and her collections. But her reaction was exactly the opposite. She sold all of the African masks and her Indian pottery. She sold some furniture and set the rest out at the curb for the trash pickup. She had the floors stripped down to natural wood, then waxed. The walls were all painted white. She ordered only enough gray steel office utility furniture for storage or essential seating. She said that soft chairs only produce boring, soft conversation. She has one single reception room with a few small tables that may be pushed together and serve for dining or conversation. The rest of the house is totally given over to grouping her sculpture and assembling new works. The sculptures that she keeps in her home seem to change constantly. She adds a box to one part, takes another away, or rearranges the total work. She sleeps on the fourth floor. Her room is nearly bare, except for the bed and a sculpture done by her son, Mike. Her clothing is neatly packed into steel cabinets.

In contrast to the austerity of her furniture, she loves clothing made from rich antique fabrics. When her first large retrospective opened at the Whitney Museum in 1967, she wore a poncho made from two Japanese tapestries of purple silk, embroidered with enormous white cranes and pink cherry blossoms. The poncho covered a flounced Mexican skirt and embroidered peasant blouse.

The Whitney retrospective contained work from all of her periods, from the terra cotta figures of the 1930s to her latest walls, done in clear plexiglass. Called *Ice Palace,* the plexiglass piece appears more like a skeleton of her sculpture. The clear pieces do not hide each other as the wooden scraps do. She used only regular geometric forms. The viewer can see through the entire structure including the outline of every piece. In 1968 she abruptly stopped work in plexiglass.

She also began to work in metal during the 1960s. At first she found it difficult, because the metal could not be glued like wood, but she soon mastered the different techniques required. In 1969 she received a grant from Princeton University to do her first steel monumental sculpture.

Louise Nevelson has created an enormous body of work. She also has generously given her time and energy to organizations that work for the rights and welfare of artists and has held national offices in these organizations. She has devoted time to councils that advise the government on artistic and cultural affairs. She traveled to Washington to participate in the National Council on Arts and Government, and she was head of the Advisory Council on Art of the National Historic Site Foundation.

Although she has experimented with other materials, she never seems to exhaust the possibilities for wood assemblage. Now in her seventies, her vitality undiminished, she is again working with black wood. She has created a series of small walls and more of the decorated, hollow columns, called *Dream Houses*. Little doors open to reveal the narrow interiors encrusted with more wooden forms. Shadowy and dark, the interiors look like secret hiding places.

In 1973 the Walker Art Center in Minneapolis organized an exhibit of Nevelson's wood sculpture, work covering three decades. A few white pieces were included, but most of the exhibit was devoted to the black works. When the sculptures were shown in San Francisco, they filled three large museum rooms. Nevelson was there for the opening. Dressed like an empress in a full-length paisley coat lined with chinchilla, she presided regally over her wood sculptures. She gave up everything to create those sculptures. But, as she herself says, she has created an empire.

Helen Frankenthaler invented a new technique, the soak-stain method, for creating her abstract expressionist paintings.

Being Oneself

HELEN FRANKENTHALER

Helen Frankenthaler and her older sister, Marjorie, dashed through the door of the sprawling, gray stone Metropolitan Museum that faced Fifth Avenue at Eighty-second Street in New York. During the early 1940s the girls often went to New York art museums together. That day Marjorie wanted Helen to see Dali's *Persistence of Memory*. When they found the painting, Helen stood quietly in front of it for a long time. The painting was a landscape, but not a usual one—it was an unreal dream-world, a bleak desert. Round pocket watches melted over a single bare branch and over a distorted face lying as pale as a weathered bone on the ground. Helen was astonished that an artist could take ordinary images like watches and transform them into something so imaginative and amazing. She remembers that this was the first time she really looked at a painting.

Later in her own paintings done after 1950, when she was a professional artist, she allowed patches of color to bend and flow like the watches in Dali's painting. But instead of using real images, she used abstract shapes. The patches of color were formed when paint was literally poured onto raw canvas that was unrolled on her studio floor. Helen Frankenthaler invented this new technique of soaking or staining color into canvas. Other painters were impressed when they saw the soft, flowing effect. They copied her soak-stain method. She became famous for her invention, which has in turn influenced the painting of other artists.

When Helen Frankenthaler saw Dali's *Persistence of Memory,* she was in her early teens. Even then she loved art in her classes at school. And she often visited the museums and galleries that were within easy walking distance of her family's New York apartment and her school. At Brearley, an exclusive girls' school, she painted still lifes of twigs, flowers, wine bottles, and eggs on a white tablecloth. She was skilled at painting them just as they looked.

After Brearley, Helen went to Dalton School, another excellent private school. Her mother wanted all three of her daughters to have the finest education possible. Helen's father, Alfred Frankenthaler, who had died when Helen was only twelve years old, had served as a justice on the New York State Supreme Court. He too had wanted his daughters to take advantage of the best educational and cultural facilities available in New York. In the private schools Helen attended, her study of art and academic subjects was thorough and intense.

At Dalton, her high school, she studied art with Rufino Tamayo, a famous Mexican muralist, who painted in the cubist style of Picasso. Helen Frankenthaler loved the bright colors he used—ochers, reds, oranges, and blues—and she used these colors also. He was an art teacher, but he was a real artist as well. His work was exhibited at Valentine Dudensing Gallery, where Helen went to see his exhibits and also paintings by modern European painters.

When she graduated from Dalton in 1945, she was only sixteen. She decided to stay in New York and continue her art studies with Tamayo. She was mastering the cubist style so well that he claimed she was his best student. While she studied with Tamayo, she often visited the old Guggenheim Museum, which was near her family's apartment on Seventy-second Street, and the Museum of Modern Art.

In March of 1946 she entered Bennington College in Bennington, Vermont. For Helen, Bennington was a perfect choice. At this small, private women's college, students are encouraged to study independently and to pursue their own interests, rather than to take four years of courses required for a degree. Since Helen Frankenthaler was already keenly interested in art, the chance to study at Bennington allowed her to concentrate on art without the distraction of other requirements. She studied painting, further increasing the skills she already possessed, and she acquired a great understanding of painting in a seminar taught by Paul Feeley.

When we look at a painting, we instinctively tend to either like it or not like it. Either it "works," or it "does not work." The artist has a similar instinctive reaction when creating her own work. A completed painting may "work" or "not work." It is most important for an artist to learn to analyze her own paintings in order to understand why they are successful or not. Once this understanding is reached, the artist can consistently create paintings that work.

Paul Feeley, who had just returned from the marines after World War II to become head of Bennington's art department, had the ability to analyze a painting and tell why it was successful. In his seminar he had reproductions of paintings by all the modern masters. He would analyze the paintings in terms of subject matter, color, size, and the artist's drawing ability. The illusion of three-dimensional space was compared to the two-dimensional design of the surface. The students also learned to look at a tiny portion of a painting and to analyze it in the same terms as the whole painting.

Helen Frankenthaler found this process of ana-lyzing a painting stimulating and exciting. The students wished the class would never end. They all came away excited and eager to attack their own work with fresh understanding. Helen was learning the structure and process underneath the seemingly magic vision of great art. With Tamayo she had learned how to paint cubist pictures. Now, in her studies with Paul Feeley, she understood the mechanics of cubist space and form.

Bennington students spend one term away from the campus as nonresident students, studying or working in their field. Art students usually chose to study at Hans Hofmann's school or at William Harrison's studio, both in New York. Although most of the students went to Hans Hofmann's school, Helen chose William Harrison. Fewer artists worked at his studio, but they were all serious and completely dedicated to their work. He instructed his students to take typewriter paper and do cubist drawings in the style of different artists. Helen used a soft greasy pencil and erased and erased until the drawing was done exactly in the style of Picasso or Braque or Gris. Often, days were spent on a single drawing. It was a way to thoroughly master and under-stand the style the artist used, much as art students of earlier decades had copied the old masters at the Louvre in Paris. While she was in New York, Helen Frankenthaler also worked on a magazine called *Art Outlook.* Reviews and art criticism appeared in this magazine.

The summer before her senior year of college, Helen Frankenthaler went to Europe. With the fresh eyes and enthusiasm of a twenty-year-old, she explored all of the major European cities. She also discovered the old masters for the first time. She studied the paintings of Titian, Rubens, and Velazquez. Exhibits of modern artists in Paris also impressed her.

During her senior year she became interested in writing and edited the college newspaper. Writers and philosophers, as well as other artists, were her friends in the exciting intellectual atmosphere of Bennington. Before the end of her senior year, she sold her first painting, a cubist still life, to an art critic on the Bennington faculty. When she graduated in June 1949, she knew that she wanted to paint professionally.

Moving back to New York, she shared a studio in a cold-water flat with Sonya Rudikoff, a Bennington friend who later became an art critic. Helen enrolled in graduate school at Columbia. She had an interesting course with Meyer Shapiro, an art historian, but she soon realized that she was in graduate school mainly to please her family. Halfway through the semester she simply stopped going to classes. She wanted to devote her time and energy entirely to painting.

She continued to paint in the cubist style, which she had thoroughly mastered, but she also became interested in the watercolors and early paintings done by Kandinsky, a Russian abstract artist. His work was exhibited at the Guggenheim Museum. Watercolors of the 1910 period appealed to her most, and she returned to the museum many times to see them. Fairy-tale landscapes, populated with fantastic creatures, were created out of transparent patches of lovely color. Sometimes the figures floated anywhere over the surface of the canvas. The figures in the painting were tied together by black lines that outlined their shape or looped around, cutting a path across the painting.

In 1950 Helen Frankenthaler was asked to organize an exhibit of paintings by former students of Paul Feeley's at a gallery on Fifty-seventh Street. As part of the publicity for the exhibit, Helen invited Clement Greenberg, a well-known art critic, to the opening. She took him around the gallery to see the art works. When he saw her cubist *Woman on a Horse,* painted while she was studying with William Harrison, he commented that it was one of the paintings he did not like. She later felt that it was an overambitious student's work. However, his opinion of her painting did not prevent them from becoming very good friends. And it was a friendship that became enormously important to Helen Frankenthaler.

Clement Greenberg knew all of the young modern artists who painted in the style of abstract expressionism in New York during the early 1950s. They are often referred to as the New York School. He introduced Helen Frankenthaler to all of these artists, and she became a part of the circle that included his friends. Like Paul Feeley, who could dissect cubism, Clement Greenberg could analyze abstract expressionist paintings. Through him, Helen acquired a deep understanding of this modern, revolutionary style.

Abstract expressionism is the style of painting in which spots, splashes, and smears of thick paint seem to sprawl over the canvas without order or meaning. At their first encounter with this type of painting, many viewers are puzzled and perhaps embarrassed by not understanding what they see. Many jokes have been made about abstract expressionism. Sometimes viewers joked that a child in nursery school could paint a splattered painting with poster paints. Or others joked that the paintings could be hung upside down and it made no difference. And indeed, many of them could be hung upside down, because the intention of the artist is to relate forms and designs on the surface of the painting,

Helen Frankenthaler, Woman on a Horse, *1950.*

not to reproduce an image that looks like a tree or a bowl of apples.

Considered in terms of modern art history, abstract expressionism is simply the next step or the logical development of the art movements that came just before it. All artists' training includes familiarity and mastery of the artistic styles and traditions of the past. But then, each artist feels a necessity to create some new dimension in his or her own work. Why paint, if you are only repeating what has been done before?

Modern art had its roots in the paintings of the Impressionists, who were interested in the effects of light and in the overall design of the painting. Some artists, like Van Gogh, who painted in the decade after the rise of impressionism, painted in an emotional style that interpreted nature in terms of their feelings. This is called expressionism, and the emotional nature of this kind of painting influenced abstract expressionism. Other post-impressionist artists, like Cezanne, painted nature in terms of its basic shape or structure. Cubism grew out of this concept. Cubism became an influential movement in modern art after 1910. After World War II the abstract expressionist painters revolted against the mathematical precision of cubism. They painted from their feelings and from nature, but they allowed the paint and their feelings to take over. Identification with natural objects became completely lost in the energetic arm movements and thick slashes of paint.

It was a revolutionary movement whose impact was as important to the art world as the landing of someone on the moon was to scientific technology. It firmly established New York as the art capital of the world. Helen Frankenthaler never had to chose Paris, as did Mary Cassatt, nor did she even briefly consider working there, as did Louise Nevelson. The shift to New York and the United States was complete.

Clement Greenberg brought Helen Frankenthaler into the center of this abstract expressionist movement. In later years she has said that it was a very exciting time to be a young artist in New York. At that time the public did not accept these modern paintings. The artists could sell little of their work, nor could they even get acceptance by art critics. But they believed in their work and in each other, and it was all they needed.

On Friday nights they used to go to the Artists' Club and to the Cedar Street Bar. All of the artists argued about and analyzed the work of two abstract artists, William DeKooning and Jackson Pollock. DeKooning applied his paint to the canvas in thick, heavy brush strokes. Some of his figures were recognizable women. Others were completely abstract shapes. Jackson Pollock was even more revolutionary. He unrolled his canvas on the floor and, attacking from all sides, allowed paint to drip onto the canvas. It might drip from a brush or from holes bored into the bottom of a paint can. In great energetic movements, he swung his arm or even his whole body over the canvas when he applied the paint. The pattern of drips on the canvas was a record of this energetic movement.

In the fall of 1951, Greenberg took Helen Frankenthaler to a Jackson Pollock exhibit. She had heard the artists endlessly discuss the paintings, but it was her first actual exposure to his work. She felt as if Clement Greenberg had pushed her into the room and said, "Swim!" She was overwhelmed. She sensed immediately the actual physical impact of the energetic swirls and dots on the enormous wall-sized canvases. Her first impression was simply that of an enormous, complicated pattern of dots and lines that webbed and looped over the surface. Later, she felt that images or symbols emerged from the seemingly accidental pattern. She felt that they enriched the painting, but she did not feel it was necessary to see "something."

Although Pollock's paintings made a deep impression on Helen Frankenthaler, she did not immediately begin to imitate them or to use his technique. She continued working in the cubist style, many times painting landscapes. She and Clement Greenberg often went to New England and painted the countryside. In the summer of 1950 she had painted a scene of Provincetown Bay when she studied at Hans Hofmann's summer school at the tip of Cape Cod. Near the end of that year, Adolph Gottlieb, a well-known painter, saw one of her paintings hanging in Clement Greenberg's apartment. Gottlieb had never heard of twenty-two-year-old Helen Frankenthaler, but he was so impressed with the painting that he chose to hang it in a group show put on by his dealer. It was the first time she was exhibited as a professional in New York.

After Helen saw Jackson Pollock's exhibit, Clement Greenberg took her to Springs, Long Island, to meet Pollock and his wife, the painter Lee Krasner. She never saw Jackson Pollock paint, but three or four times during the weekend all of them would walk to the studio, which was in a barn behind the house. Some of the canvases were rolled up, some tacked to the wall, others spread out on the floor.

Walking around all four sides of the canvas and looking straight down into the painting, Helen Frankenthaler saw how radical this new technique was. What made the greatest impression on her was not the drip method of painting, but the technique of painting the canvas on the floor. When an artist paints at an easel, there is always a top and a bottom, a left and a right side to the painting. Even when the artist paints a surface abstract design, he or she is still looking straight at the canvas and paints in terms of the edges. But when the canvas is unrolled on the floor, the artist can approach it from any side, giving equal importance to any view. After the painting is completed, the canvas is tacked over a stretcher. Then the canvas may be cropped and the edges of the painting drawn into the painted portion.

The possibilities for using this technique excited Helen, but she did not yet apply it to her own work. During the summer of 1952 she went to Nova Scotia and Cape Breton to paint. She worked outdoors in water-color on folding easel equipment. She was particularly impressed with the thickly wooded hills that dropped directly down to the water's edge.

When she returned to New York in the fall, she seemed ready to use Pollock's technique to create her own work. She bought a bolt of cotton duck from a sail maker, since art stores did not have canvas large enough for the paintings she wished to create. She un-rolled it on the floor of her Twenty-third Street studio.

Unlike Pollock, who used thick enamels that tended to stay on the surface, Helen thinned her paint with turpentine, and it soaked right into the cloth when she poured it on. As the painting progressed, it appeared to be colored canvas, rather than thicks drips of paint on the surface. Pollock used black and white; she chose lovely, luminous pastels—the colors of Kandinsky's watercolors that she had admired at the Guggenheim Museum.

The thinned paint was not controllable, and getting the right shapes, or preventing the edges of colors from

bleeding into each other and becoming muddy, was difficult. Then, after she had poured and created shapes and
swirls, she had to decide when to stop adding colors and
shapes. Finally satisfied with the appearance, she stopped
before the images became too large or before too many
overpowered the canvas. This beautiful, luminous pastel
painting, called *Mountains and Sea,* was in her soak-stain
method, her invention that added an entirely new dimension to modern painting.

While *Mountains and Sea* is not a traditional
landscape of the shoreline, Frankenthaler says that the
mountains and sea of Nova Scotia were in her arm when
she painted it. The pale delicate shapes look like images
shimmering below clear water. Reproductions of the
painting now appear in modern art history books as a
landmark of the soak-stain technique. Helen Frankenthaler was then twenty-four years old.

Mountains and Sea was first exhibited at Tibor de
Nagy Gallery in New York, where Helen had yearly
one-man exhibits beginning in 1951. Located under the
noisy Third Avenue El, the gallery was owned by John
Myers. He exhibited the work of young, unknown artists
who painted in abstract styles. Exhibiting unknown
artists required great faith and willingness to take great
financial risks. Many young artists never become famous
or even successful enough to sell their paintings. But
dealers willing to risk their money and reputations are
necessary to young artists for financial and emotional
support. The art dealers of new work also change trends
in the art world by revealing new ideas.

After discovering her soak-stain technique in late
1952, Frankenthaler produced several other works in
quick succession. She tends to work in energetic cycles,
creating many works within a short period. Her impulse

Helen Frankenthaler, Mountains and Sea, *1952.*

Helen Frankenthaler in her studio in New York in 1975.

to keep changing and experimenting is strong, so the paintings after *Mountains and Sea* appear with a changed format. In *Open Wall* she allowed the color to stain and run off the edge of the canvas. It gives the illusion of looking at only a portion of a gently billowing silky curtain whose dimensions extend far beyond the edge of the canvas. She achieves this effect by having the canvas tacked over wooden stretchers after it is painted on the floor. In this way she can crop the edge of the canvas at any place she chooses, including the middle of a stained area. Our own imagination fills in the rest, allowing the image to go beyond the edge of her already large wall-sized paintings.

Another beautiful painting of this period is called *Shatter*. One soft result of pouring thinned oil paint onto raw canvas was that the turpentine seeped farther into the cloth than the pigment and created a turpentine halo around the colored areas. This softened and unified her pastel colors and eliminated any definite line between the white canvas and colored paint. *Shatter* demonstrates this unified quality. It is impossible to tell where she started, what color she chose first, or where the last bit of color was applied. She discards any paintings that look as if she started with a certain color, added another, then another. It must look "as if it were born in a minute," she says.

During the mid-1950s Frankenthaler made several summer trips to Europe. Like other artists, she traveled not only to have a vacation, but also to view art works. Art was not a career that she abandoned during a trip—it was her life. When she traveled abroad, she went to study the old masters. She viewed paintings in museums, statues in cathedrals, and Renaissance art treasures in Italian hill towns. Many of the paintings she did in her studio after these trips have titles that reflect her journeys. *Round Trip, Europa,* and *Passport* were some of her choices. She names her paintings only after they are completed, and then only for the purpose of differentiating the paintings from each other. She claims that names are easier to remember than numbers. Sometimes the titles relate to nothing at all in the painting. Other times images or colors may suggest a place, a mood, or an experience which then inspires the title.

Like Mary Cassatt, Helen Frankenthaler discovered the work of Peter Paul Rubens in Europe. She painted *Venus and the Mirror,* a tribute to a portrait that Rubens painted of his wife as Venus. Of course, her stained canvas looks nothing at all like the romantic Rubens portrait, but the freshness of the sketch and the enormous size of her paintings are qualities she shares with Rubens. When Rubens painted, he had the advantage of sketching before he painted, either in preliminary drawings or directly on the canvas before applying paint. When Frankenthaler sketched, it was directly onto the canvas with the poured paint.

In the early 1950s she shared her studio with other artists. But by 1955 she had chosen to rent an apartment and studio by herself on West End Avenue. It was a lonely period for her. Her mother died that year, and in the next year Jackson Pollock was killed in an automobile accident. In spite of living through an unhappy personal period, she had one of her great spurts of creativity about 1957. Some of the paintings strike the viewer as light hearted, almost humorous. She seemed to have achieved great skill in suggesting images and completing a painting with a minimum of color or paint on the canvas.

In *Toward a New Climate,* an orange sun with

paint splatters radiating out shines happily over half of the canvas. The other half has vertical feathered stains of the same orange paint. The area between remains unstained. Two other paintings, *Eden* and *Seven Types of Ambiguity,* also have happy suns on the canvas. In *Seven Types of Ambiguity* the pale tans and yellows seem flooded with a source of light that springs from the canvas itself.

Critics speak of the "ambiguity of space" in her painting. Since she stains the color into the canvas itself, there is no background or foreground in the painting. Yet, when the viewer looks at the paintings, some of the images float over the surface; others seem to recede in the background. If we close our eyes, and then look at the painting freshly, the images can be reversed —those previously on the surface have receded into the background. This quality can keep a painting fresh and constantly changing for the viewer. It is one of the qualities that makes a painting "work."

Jacob's Ladder, another of the 1957 paintings, won an international award in 1959—a first prize at the Biennale de Paris. A ladder with square blocks marking each rung marches straight up the center of the canvas.

Among the painters that Helen Frankenthaler knew in New York was Robert Motherwell. Like Jackson Pollock, he was considered a "first generation" abstract expressionist and had established a major reputation. In 1958 she painted *Before the Caves* with the numerals 173 scattered throughout the painting. It was the address of Motherwell's brownstone house in New York. Helen and Robert were married in April of 1958.

They traveled to France and Spain, where they spent several months on their honeymoon, living in a rented villa at St. Jean de Luz. They visited the cave paintings in northern Spain, the oldest examples of art in the western world. They also visited the house of the painter El Greco in Toledo, a town near Madrid. Frankenthaler titled one of her paintings *The Courtyard of El Greco's House.* Instead of splatters and lines of paint swirling through the canvas, the paint is poured on in larger, thicker areas that suggest the heavy outlines of a thick-walled Spanish house.

After the Motherwells returned to New York, they lived in the brownstone house in the East Nineties numbered 173, where they still live today. Helen brought to their home the art works she had collected before her marriage and added them to the things Robert had collected. Of course, the couple have continued to add paintings and sculpture to their collection.

Many of the art works are small bronze statues that rest on tables or on the floor throughout the comfortable living room. Statues by Degas and Rodin are some of Frankenthaler's favorites. In the hallway, African straw masks hang beside English landscapes and Clement Greenberg's lyric oils. The walls are covered with their own paintings and those of their friends.

The couple returned from their Mediterranean honeymoon inspired to decorate their house in the colors of homes in that part of the world. The walls are chalk white, a fine background for their large modern paintings; the ceilings are the azure color of the sea; and the doors are dark walnut. Their tasteful, comfortable home and their collections have often been featured in articles in decorating magazines.

In 1958 Helen Frankenthaler had a painting, *Lorelei,* chosen for an exhibit entitled "Nature in Abstraction" held at the Whitney Museum. This exhibit has become a landmark in modern art, much the same as

Frankenthaler's painting *Mountains and Sea.*

Another symbol of her growing reputation in New York was her switch from yearly exhibits at Tibor de Nagy Gallery to Andre Emmerich Gallery in 1959. Andre Emmerich, who exhibits the work of established artists, has been her dealer ever since.

The first retrospective of her work was held in 1960 at the Jewish Museum. The paintings in the retrospective recorded her decade-long artistic career from the cubist-influenced works of her student days through all the variations of the soak-stain paintings. Perhaps seeing all of the work together inspired her to change her technique, and during 1961 she began to prime her canvases. This changed the appearance of the paintings: Instead of soaking into the cloth, the paint tended to ride on top. As a result, the colors appeared brighter, more intense. She concentrated the images in large blot patterns toward the center of the painting.

This change in technique heralded one of her very active periods. She continued to pour or lay on color areas on a canvas that rested on the floor. She might create a shape by spreading the paint with a sponge or a brush. After she worked on the floor, she hung the canvas on the wall to study the effect. Then she sometimes put it back on the floor and continued to work in more shapes. The final step was choosing how much of the canvas area would be tacked over the stretcher. Her paintings continued to be very large; often each side ranged eight feet or more in length.

In 1962 she again altered her technique by switching from oils to acrylics. Since acrylic paints use water as a base, they dry much more rapidly than oils. Also, acrylic colors have a more dense, bright look. At first Frankenthaler found it difficult to control the image she wanted, because the paint dried so quickly. Without the turpentine halo of oil paints, the edges of her colors were more sharp. She began to run color areas together to produce softer, more blended edges.

After Frankenthaler began using acrylics, she also began to cover most of the canvas with paint, often in closely related hues. *The Bay,* one of her earliest acrylics, painted in 1963, may have been inspired by her summers in Cape Cod. During the 1960s, Helen Frankenthaler had studios in Provincetown each summer. In *The Bay* a large mass of blue floats in the center of the painting.

Frankenthaler was asked if she had a plan for these abstract paintings before she started to pour the paint onto the canvas. She answered that instead of some plan for shape or form, she started working with three different shades of a color, like the blues of *The Bay,* to see what would "happen." The blue mass floats above a large colored section of gray and green. The point between the gray and green looks like a horizon. The painting is not a realistic picture of the sea, but its colors suggest Cape Cod Bay in the summer.

During 1963 she returned briefly to oils and the soak-stain technique, and she stretched these finished canvases in an interesting manner. Instead of having the top surface of the canvas facing out, she had the back side showing. The imprint of the floorboards from her Eighty-third Street studio add a regular slatted pattern to the painting, crossing the painting horizontally or vertically. The colors seep through the cloth like a soft mist. She experimented in this style several times, and then she returned to bright acrylics which she continues to use today.

Using the brighter paints, she began to put the colors on the canvas like nesting boxes. In 1964 she painted *Interior Landscape,* where the central patch of bright green explodes out of its box at one point, cuts through the yellow, and nearly reaches the edge of the canvas. This thrusting out seemed to symbolize the end of the boxed colors. In an interview with Henry Geldzahler, Frankenthaler was asked why she changed her style so often. She said that she feels she must try something new simply to "move on." Her pattern of work, since the invention of the soak-stain technique, seems to be to develop an idea and then move on to another rather than risk repetition.

By the mid-1960s, Frankenthaler's work was being shown not only at Andre Emmerich, her New York dealer, but also at Galerie Lawrence in Paris. Lawrence Rubin, owner of the Paris gallery, was one of the first dealers in France to show the younger "second generation" abstract expressionist American painters. He was a close friend of Clement Greenberg, and he exhibited the work of painters who were of special interest to Greenberg. In 1964 Helen Frankenthaler also had an exhibit in London. During the period of these exhibits in Europe she often traveled abroad to see them.

In spite of these frequent trips to Europe, the move to Cape Cod each summer, and her creative output, she still managed to teach art on a part-time basis. Perhaps her interest in teaching stems from the excellence of her own education. Teaching gives her the opportunity for contact with the intellectual atmosphere of universities. She first taught in 1957 in an adult education program on Long Island, organized by artists who exhibited at Tibor de Nagy Gallery. From 1958 to 1961 she taught at the New York University School of Education. In 1962 she taught at Hunter College in New York, and the following year she began to serve on the Fulbright

Selection Committee. Fulbright scholars are given grants to study or teach abroad. In turn, scholars from other countries are brought to universities in this country to study or teach.

In 1966 Frankenthaler was chosen to represent the United States in the Venice Biennale. This invitation to exhibit in the World's Fair of modern art pointed to her stature as an artist of the first rank. The work she hung in the Biennale spanned all the periods of her career, the early *Mountains and Sea,* some of the bright acrylics that were stained on every inch of canvas, and her latest work, *One O'Clock.* In her newest style she stained the canvas at the edge and left the center totally bare, like some vast openness viewed from the window of a spaceship.

The following year, she was again asked to represent her country at a world's fair, Canada's Expo 67 in Montreal. In this case she was commissioned to do a large work especially for the fair. She purchased more than thirty feet of canvas for the project and unrolled it on the floor of her sunny studio. She walked around the canvas, just looking at it, for nearly two weeks. Then she decided to fly to Paris for a week and go to a Picasso show. When she came home, she was much more relaxed and could start to pour and blend her paints on the raw canvas. She had to physically get right into the painting, because she could not reach the center from the edge. "I just walked in on the red," she said.

When Frankenthaler wanted to view the painting hanging as it would at the exposition in Montreal, she rented an old movie theater that had a large enough stage. The painting hung thirty feet down from the high ceiling, and it measured sixteen feet across.

An enormous banner of red color shimmered down

the center of the canvas. It demonstrated the trend in her paintings at the end of the 1960s to large, bold, simple shapes stained over large areas of canvas. Absolutely gone were the splatters, swirling lines, or whimsical effects of the paintings of the 1950s. The trend to simple, monumental shapes grew in her work until, finally, she did a painting consisting of one bold diagonal path of sienna over the canvas, the single brush stroke of a giant. These paintings seem more serious and controlled than her earlier works. This style has continued through her yearly exhibits of the 1970s. The large shapes now may cover the entire canvas, with smaller, darker lines of paint drawn over the top.

Exhibiting in the Venice Biennale and Expo 67 showed that Helen Frankenthaler was not only a major artist in her own country, but one of international renown as well. She had earned this reputation in only fifteen years from the time she had exhibited *Mountains and Sea* as a young unknown artist at Tibor de Nagy Gallery. For someone only thirty-eight years old, it was a remarkable achievement. In that same year, 1967, she also began to teach at the School of Art and Architecture at Yale University, and in 1968 she became a Fellow of Calhoun College at Yale. The students in her classes found a talented, successful artist who shared her ideas in well-chosen words.

Art schools and other universities began to recognize Frankenthaler's achievements. The Philadelphia Academy of Fine Arts, Skidmore College, and the Albert Einstein School of Medicine were among the schools to present her with awards.

Another important measure of an artist's reputation is recognition by a major museum in the form of a retrospective of the artist's work, and in 1969 the Whitney

Museum held such an exhibit. It was a milestone for her career, in that it seemed to bring her a wider audience and recognition from a greater range of people. While her work in the early 1950s grew out of abstract expressionism, then the most popular art movement in New York, the direction of her work in the 1960s departed from the styles popular among artists of that decade. Movements with names like pop art, op art, and minimal art gained acceptance by artists, critics, art magazines, and certain gallery owners that make up the New York art scene. Helen Frankenthaler's work remained unaffected by these trends or fads. She continued to develop and improvise on her soak-stain technique.

A term consistently applied to her work throughout her career has been *lyric*. Sometimes she has been called a "poetic painter." Yet these labels are hard to pin down. She claims that she used to wonder if the lyricism that others saw in her work came from her being a woman. But she goes on to say that looking at her paintings as if they were painted by a woman is a side issue.

The creation of a serious painting is difficult and complicated for all painters. "One must be oneself, whatever." This statement by the artist perhaps best characterizes her work and the work of all great artists. Helen Frankenthaler is "being herself" in the beautiful soak-stained color paintings that we can see in museums throughout the United States.

Energetic Suzanne Jackson has been a dancer, a poet, and a teacher, in addition to her ongoing career as a painter.

Reality Versus Fantasy

SUZANNE JACKSON

In her book *What I Love,* a collection of poetry and paintings, Suzanne Jackson writes,

> My art deals with reality
> versus fantasy—aloneness
> versus loneliness . . . What I
> paint attempts to express the
> conflicts within the mind,
> conflicts of choices—of loves,
> —of sensitivities searching,
> ordering, "freeing" oneself
> toward some continuous
> cycle of rediscovering who,
> in fact, I really might be.

Who is Suzanne Jackson? She is a painter who also writes poetry. She is a young woman. Now in her thirties, she was born on January 30, 1944. A former ballet dancer, she moves with the grace of a flamingo, a bird she sometimes includes in her paintings. She studied ballet and danced professionally before she devoted all of her considerable energy to painting.

Her paintings depict natural forms. Flowers, birds, and human faces, limbs, or bodies float in a dreamlike space. Many of her paintings combine abstract shapes and clouds of color with real images. As she writes in her poem, her paintings are an expression of "reality versus fantasy."

Like Helen Frankenthaler, Suzanne Jackson paints on the floor. But her canvas is stretched, and her images represent real things. Her figures are more controlled than the abstract shapes of poured and soaked paint. Suzanne brushes on many layers of paints to produce beautiful, soft colors and an interplay of paint layers in a style similar to the old masters. No other modern painter employs this technique; it is her invention. And the airiness and open quality of her paintings are unique.

The human figures that Suzanne Jackson depicts in her paintings are black people, but her work does not present the problems of black ghetto dwellers that appear in the works of some other modern black artists. Perhaps this reflects the fact that Suzanne Jackson did not grow up in the South or in a large city of the United States.

Her parents decided to move to Alaska from San Francisco, when Suzanne was in the fourth grade, because of the business opportunities available in the frontier atmosphere there. Her father worked in construction, owned a real estate office, and supplied American military bases with bread. Suzanne remembers that her father always had more than one job at a time. Families living in Alaska were very close. Isolated during the long, cold winters and having only limited goods and services, people learned to help each other.

When they arrived in Fairbanks, the Jacksons bought a small house. Each summer Mr. Jackson added one room, then another, until their house grew into a large, comfortable home. House building was often a cooperative event, with neighbors helping each other. An only child, Suzanne played Scrabble and Monopoly with her parents during the many dark hours of the arctic winter nights. She also helped bake the bread for her father's business. When he drove to the military bases to deliver the bread, a trip of four hundred miles that had to be made twice a week, Suzanne and her mother ran the real estate office.

Because the family was separated from Suzanne's grandmother, who lived in Saint Louis, where Suzanne was born, Suzanne wrote letters and drew pictures to mail to her. It was the earliest art work she did. She continues to enjoy writing as well as painting, and she has produced two books of poems and paintings.

The school Suzanne attended did not have regular art classes, but when she was in the seventh grade, a teacher did come into the school to teach watercolors. Already thinking about being a painter, Suzanne remembers copying pictures out of *National Geographic*. But the best subjects were right outside her windows. The mountains, evergreen trees, rivers, and birds provide the grandest subjects for any artist interested in landscape painting. More artists live in Alaska in proportion to the population than in any other state.

Suzanne was busy with outside activities, one of which was tracking birds for the Audubon Society. Birds frequently appear in her paintings, perhaps a carry-over from the days when she could recognize the coloration and calls of many birds in the far north.

In addition, Suzanne studied ballet, and in high school she danced with a professional company. Sometimes they performed jazz and Spanish dances, as well as ballet.

In high school she worked on the yearbook and the school newspaper. She briefly considered being a commercial artist, but when her yearbook drawings had to be changed to suit the editor, she decided commercial art was not for her. If she had an idea, she wanted to carry it out in her own way, not adapt it to the needs of a newspaper or magazine. Although the high school did not have art classes, the students were encouraged to pursue their individual interests and talents.

Suzanne received her first oil paints as a Christmas gift from her father when she was sixteen years old, and she remembers painting in every spare moment after that. After reading about Nigeria, she decided to paint a turbaned Nigerian girl, and she entered the portrait in an art exhibit. The competition was for professional artists, but Suzanne's painting won first prize, even though she had never had an art lesson in her life. Then she entered the painting in the county fair, and it won first prize there also.

Suzanne graduated from high school in 1961, and that summer she taught dancing in Fairbanks. She earned enough to buy her airplane ticket to San Francisco, where she entered San Francisco State College, now California State University at San Francisco.

At San Francisco State she registered in both art and dance classes. High school had given her an education; now she was ready to pursue her training in art and dance. San Francisco State's art program had been very unstructured before Suzanne arrived. Teachers encouraged the loose painting of Jackson Pollock and other abstract expressionists without requiring students to take drawing classes or learn how to solve other problems of painting and sculpture.

This policy had changed by the time Suzanne enrolled. The approach to painting was more disciplined and traditional. Each semester, art students had to take a set of three classes. Design, sculpture, and watercolor painting might be followed by drawing, oil painting, and another phase of sculpture. She remembers liking sculpture. The class went to the dump and found cast-offs that they assembled into sculptures. Suzanne also worked in plaster. Sometimes she painted her sculpture in pale, washlike colors, and white. The size of her three-dimensional work grew and grew, until it got too big—and then she abruptly stopped work in sculpture.

In painting classes, the instructors posed problems for the students to solve. Students learned to compose a painting with a certain number of figures, how to relate colors to each other for certain effects, and how to create three-dimensional space. One instructor in particular, Wesley Chamberlain, made her work and rework the painting until she had "solved the problem." Now that Suzanne is a professional artist, she mails him an invitation whenever she has an opening for an exhibit. He also taught her to paint on the floor, a practice she has continued. Watercolors and the thinned acrylic paints that Suzanne now uses must be painted on a flat surface; the paint would drip and run over the surface if the painting were set up on an easel.

The most important part of the art program at San Francisco State occurred during Suzanne's final semester there. Students majoring in art and working toward a professional painting degree spent an extra semester in school to earn their regular degree. During this semester students painted on their own in the college studio, just like professional artists. They were expected to apply the techniques learned in four years of classes. After students completed their paintings in the college studio, they went to a professor for criticism.

In her last semester working in the college studio, Suzanne painted four figure studies in watercolor and ink on canvas. Although acrylic paints were introduced to her this last year in college, she rejected them at that time because she thought they were too flat and dull. In her four paintings she used white extensively, pale red white, blue white, and yellow white. (White is nearly always tinted with some other color.) The people that Suzanne painted looked like popular figures of the mid-1960s— the Beatles, model Jean Shrimpton, and photographer David Bailey. When she finished, she studied the paintings. She did not know if she had created cartoons, or portraits, or paintings. Did they "work?" With some anxiety she took them to a professor to be criticized. He went over them with Suzanne in detail. Finally, he concluded that they not only "worked," but that they also were original and excellent paintings.

Suzanne has used various tones of white, as she did in those four paintings, again and again. Her most recent work as a professional artist attacks the problem of using different hues of white, painted in many thin layers over the canvas.

During the years that Suzanne earned her degree in art at San Francisco State, she also danced professionally with the Pacific Ballet Company. At school she danced in all of the shows put on by the music and drama departments. Like her father, she seems to have the energy to do more than one thing at a time. During her last year in college she also taught art in an elementary school and she did some part-time modeling. In the early 1960s it was still difficult for a black woman to be accepted as a model. "You had to look like a white woman," she says. But that has changed.

By the time she had graduated from San Francisco State in January 1966, Suzanne was already married. But the marriage lasted only a brief time and then was annulled. A short time later she heard about a dance company in Sacramento that needed two black ballet dancers. She boarded the plane the following morning for the short flight, passed the audition, and became a member of the Music Circus. Exhausted after the years in college and after the annullment of her marriage, she needed a change and she did not paint at all during the following year. She regards the year with the dance company as a transitional period in her life.

Music Circus presented two shows, *Carousel* and *Showboat,* in a tent that seated eighteen hundred people. They danced in Sacramento and Fresno and then went to Los Angeles, where they prepared for a Latin American tour under the sponsorship of the State Department. They changed the name of the company to Music Theatre U.S.A. when they performed in Latin America.

Music Theatre U.S.A. went to Mexico City, then to Guadalajara, and eventually to all of the major cities of South America. *Showboat* and *Carousel* were presented to show a sample of American theater and music to the people in Latin America. At that time there was anti-American feeling in South America, and there were protests against the dance company. In Uruguay Suzanne remembers tanks surrounding the theater and attempts to cut off the electricity. They just missed a revolution in Cordoba and discovered bullet holes riddling the walls.

During the tour she had little opportunity to see the countries or meet the people. Dancers, like athletes, need to conserve their energy and keep their bodies in excellent form. They danced every night except Monday. When she did have the opportunity to meet some of the people, they never believed that she was from the United States because of her dark skin. Since her Spanish was not perfect, they assumed that she was a native of Brazil, where Portuguese is spoken. They did not believe that black people lived in North America.

In early 1967 Suzanne returned to California, ready to get on with life. She moved to Los Angeles. Being a dancer she felt there were opportunities for work in television and films. She went expecting to do more theater, but it turned out that she did less.

Eager to start painting again, she looked for a studio where she could paint as well as live. A real estate agent directed her to a store front on Temple Street. When she saw the small room, she said that it would not do; she could never paint in such a tiny space. Then they walked through a small hole at the side of the room, and like Alice wandering down the rabbit hole, they followed a passage that led to a large underground area. They were in the basement of a large Victorian house. She remembers the rooms were arranged like beads strung on a necklace. The living room led to a bedroom, which led to a kitchen. The workroom, which later became her studio, was the final room in the chain. The basement rooms became her first studio and comfortable living quarters.

During the school year in 1967, Suzanne began teaching first grade at Ninety-fifth Street School. Her students were those who had difficulty in getting along in other classrooms. Teaching the restless youngsters proved a challenge, but Suzanne managed. She liked using art as a way to teach other skills and facts. The children, who could not concentrate on reading assignments, loved to draw, paint, and paste.

She herself returned to her art studies by taking classes at Otis Art Institute. A Saturday watercolor class taught by Noel Quinn proved to be her most interesting class. Quinn introduced new ideas like applying color on top of color. He also gave his students practical hints, such as suggesting that they buy watercolors in tubes. On her own, she painted in watercolors and tried some of the new techniques.

During her first year in Los Angeles, she moved to a Spanish style house on a hill. Again she set up her studio in her living quarters. She speaks of this studio as a "small space." The size and shape of the room she paints in seems to affect her work. She seems sensitive to the "space" of her studio.

During the summer of 1968 she studied drawing with Charles White at Otis. He proved to be one of the most inspirational teachers she ever had. A black man himself, he claimed that no matter what figure he drew, when he finished, the figure had the features of a black person. Famous for his studies of black people, he encouraged Suzanne to draw black figures. He shared his experiences as a poor, struggling student at the Art Institute of Chicago with his students. "He is a beautiful person," she says. After she began to exhibit her own work, her paintings appeared with his drawings at Chaffee College and University of the Pacific.

The summer she studied with Charles White, she entered two paintings in the Watts Art Festival. Watts is the center of the black community in Los Angeles. The paintings were two of the figure studies in watercolor and ink done during her last year at San Francisco State. Some people visiting the Watts festival from the Laguna Beach Art Museum singled out her work and invited Suzanne to exhibit in a show of black artists at

Laguna Beach. It was her first opportunity to exhibit in a museum and her first invitational exhibit. She sold a painting of a little boy from this exhibit.

Then her Spanish house on the hill was up for sale, and she had to hunt for new living and work quarters. She found rooms in the Granada Buildings. Copied from actual buildings in Granada, Spain, they are used as

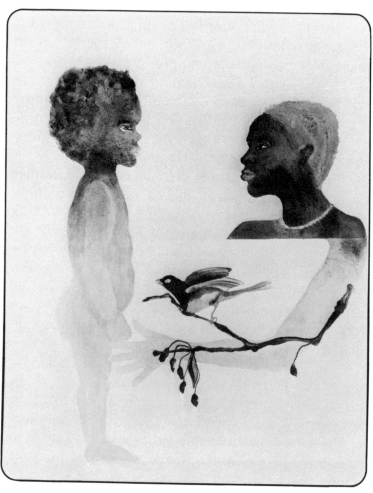

Suzanne Jackson, Shango, He Is My Love, *1972.*

European style shops with living quarters on an upper floor above the shop. Suzanne loved the old-world look of the fish ponds, the tiles, and the ornate elevator. She rented space and opened a gallery on the first floor. In honor of Alfred Stieglitz's 291 Gallery, she named her shop Gallery 32, the number of her suite of rooms.

For the first exhibition in the gallery, she invited three friends to show their paintings. She drew up mailing lists from people she knew in the theater; she found names in the telephone book; and she had public service announcements put on the radio. Then on March 19, 1969, two hundred people came to the opening. It was considered a fine success for a brand new gallery.

During the time that she was opening her gallery, she was still teaching school. But on weekends and in the summer, she concentrated on her own painting. She began to paint flowers, trees, vines, and other natural forms in oil and watercolor on small canvases. They began to cover the entire walls of her studio from floor to ceiling.

During the first six months Suzanne sold only a few paintings from the gallery. She covered expenses with her teacher's salary. Then, in the fall of 1969, she exhibited paintings by Dan Concholar, another young artist, whose work is found in several museum collections. Nearly all of Concholar's paintings sold, starting a period of self-support for the gallery. At that time she was a member of the Black Arts Council of Los Angeles. She sponsored a special Christmas exhibit with the Black Arts Council.

Some of Suzanne's friends interested her in exhibiting art for political causes. When she was in college she had sometimes joined civil rights marches, a form of the protest movement of the 1960s. Now she felt that she could reach more people by exhibiting political art in her gallery. She thought it was more effective for her than going out in the streets and demonstrating. During 1969 and early 1970, Gallery 32 became known as a "people's" gallery.

But eventually Suzanne drifted away from political and civil rights activities. "I think the movement is me," she now says. Yet her paintings portray black figures and faces in great beauty and dignity, so that anyone viewing them is touched by the noble quality of their humanity. Her delicate, poetic paintings speak louder than the harsh words and images of protest art.

During this period she was sometimes asked by her friends why she herself did not paint guns, police dogs, or other threats that often confront people who live in ghettos. She answered that she painted dreams and fantasies, for they are as much a part of the people as the problems they encounter in their everyday living. But she feels that raising these issues was good for her because it caused her to question her art. She concluded that what she did was valid and, for her, more important than political activities.

In 1969, she left her teaching job to concentrate on her own painting and on running Gallery 32. She also got an art dealer for her paintings, an enormously important step toward her ability to support herself by her art work. She was introduced to her dealer by Bernie Casey, a friend who also served on the Black Arts Council. Besides being an artist, Casey also played professional football with the Los Angeles Rams. He saw her small paintings that hung from floor to ceiling, corner to corner, and he asked teasingly what she intended to do with them. He thought she could sell them, so he took her to his dealer, Ankrum Gallery in Los Angeles.

Suzanne was immediately impressed with the gallery, and she felt ready to show her work. Also, Ankrum Gallery agreed to take five of her paintings. Shortly afterward, Joseph Hirshorn, one of the foremost art collectors in the United States, bought some of her work. One of these paintings is now exhibited in the Palm Springs Museum, where Hirshorn serves as a trustee. Suzanne was excited, even shocked, when she learned about the sale. Even now, after selling three hundred paintings, she still finds it exciting to know that someone likes her paintings well enough to buy them.

Although her work sold well during 1970, Ankrum Gallery did not give Suzanne a one-woman exhibit for nearly two years. Sometimes Suzanne felt that they were testing her. Not only was she young, she also had recently married, and, near the end of 1970, she was expecting a baby. She had felt that she was being tested at San Francisco State also. A young woman artist was not taken seriously by others. Everyone expected that eventually such women married, had families, and gave up painting. Sometimes she felt that "she would show them," but later she decided that it was not necessary. She painted for herself. She feels that she does not need to prove to anyone that she is serious or liberated.

By the time Suzanne's art work became available at Ankrum Gallery, she had switched to acrylic paints instead of oils and watercolors, and she paints exclusively in acrylics now.

Her own gallery was doing very well during 1970, but Suzanne felt it was time to change its system of showing art work. Perhaps it was time to move out into the community, with the paintings displayed in a van or in a boxcar. She felt she needed to change from repeating exhibition after exhibition within the same gallery.

Suzanne and her husband were also drifting apart by the end of 1970. Deciding to close the gallery permanently, she moved to San Francisco. Immediately after she arrived, she painted several small canvases for a Christmas exhibit at a small gallery in Los Angeles. Then she stopped painting for several months, the only time she has stopped painting since the year she danced in Latin America. Like that year, it was a period of transition. Her son was born—named Rafiki for his father even though the marriage was now ending. She returned to Los Angeles to act in a play written by a friend and presented by the Watts Writers' Workshop.

In the late summer of 1971 she was invited to be in an exhibit of black artists at the Oakland Museum. She decided it was time to be involved again, with her own work and with other people. She set up a studio in the basement of her parents' home and completed three paintings. Others were borrowed from Ankrum Gallery and her collectors. Reviews singled out her paintings of flowers, birds, and human figures for their quietly poetic and delicate qualities.

After the Oakland exhibit she continued to paint steadily in the studio in her parents' home. She had a productive routine of spending many hours a day painting and yet having time to be with Rafiki when he was awake. Her parents helped her care for him.

At the beginning of 1972, her boundless energy again bubbled up. In addition to her painting, she agreed to be the arts coordinator for Black Expo '72. Held in the Civic Center of San Francisco, Expo was meant to offer opportunities to black people and to show their accomplishments to everyone. It was a display of commercial and artistic exhibits. Suzanne gathered the work of 169 artists who lived all over the United States. She also arranged an exhibit of children's work. Well-organized and efficient, Suzanne had set up a schedule of things to be done in February, although Expo did not open until September of 1972. She recalls being gone from six in the morning until two the following morning on some days. Other times she had to travel to contact the artists. Then the night before the exhibit opened, she hung nearly the entire show herself.

Besides coordinating art work for Expo and her own painting, she taught painting at Stanford University during the summer of 1972. Also that year, her book *What I Love,* a volume of her poetry and some of her paintings, appeared. Creating one of the paintings, *Grandparents,* which now hangs in the living room of her parents' home, was a labor of love for Suzanne. She modeled the two figures in the painting on an old, faded photograph of her grandparents. Her grandmother stands quietly in the background, her grandfather in front of her. On the front surface of the painting two sets of hands reach out to them, as though reaching through time as well as space.

On the day that Black Expo closed, Suzanne boarded the four o'clock plane for Los Angeles. She arrived an hour later, got a cab, and went directly to Ankrum Gallery for the opening of her first one-woman exhibit. All of the work in this exhibit had been completed during the previous year while she was involved in Expo and teaching at Stanford.

Although natural forms like flowers, birds, and rainbows appear in these paintings, they are not inspired by nature. They are Suzanne Jackson's vision and her dreams, both daydreams and dreams at night. When we view them, we are invited into her world. Some of the symbols, like the rainbow, have appeared over and over again in African art. Suzanne does not copy them intentionally; she believes that inspiration for them springs from a spiritual continuity she shares with her Egyptian ancestors.

In spite of the fact that she paints from this inner inspiration, Suzanne does not place her images on the canvas haphazardly. She remembers the lessons of design, color, and composition learned at San Francisco State. She says that sometimes she paints a vine or a bird that is absolutely beautiful. But the next morning when she looks at the canvas, she knows the vine or the bird has to be painted out for the sake of the whole painting. Like the poet who crosses out a metaphor that does not fit the poem, she eliminates any part of a painting that does not fit into the whole composition.

Another influence from her training at San Francisco State is the responsibility Suzanne feels to treat her canvas well so that the painting will not fade or deteriorate in time. She believes the canvas should be primed and well covered. "When someone buys a painting for several hundred dollars," she says, "the artist has a responsibility to see that it will last."

At the time of the one-woman exhibit, Suzanne decided to move back to Los Angeles. She wanted to be closer to Ankrum Gallery, since they had represented her so well. This last exhibit had been a success, since nearly all of the paintings sold. A very large studio, an entire floor of forty-eight hundred square feet, became available, and Suzanne rented it. She was excited at the prospect of working in this large space, which covered a whole city block on Jefferson Boulevard.

In her larger studio, the size of her paintings seemed to expand. One, a triptych—that is, a painting done on three panels—was twelve feet long and four feet high. A new looseness developed in all her work. Images or fragments of images float out of clouds of color. Spreading her canvases on the floor, she often works on several at one time. Sometimes she likes to listen to records while she paints. Other times she needs total silence.

During 1973 her work was featured in several exhibits. At Chaffee College she exhibited with her friend, Bernie Casey, and with Charles White, the instructor she had admired so greatly. She had a one-woman show in Fresno, but she was disappointed when none of the paintings sold. Later they were shipped to Ankrum Gallery and were sold easily.

Through 1973 her paintings had appeared in exhibits almost exclusively in California. By 1974, the reputation of the young artist had spread to New York and the rest of the east. One of her paintings was shown at Cornell University in an exhibit of black artists. Then Suzanne was invited to be represented and exhibited by a New York dealer, the Just Above Mid-town Gallery. Linda Bryant, director of this gallery, came to California to view the work of several artists. She saw Suzanne's paintings and invited her to become one of the gallery's artists. Just Above Mid-town Gallery is located on Fifty-seventh Street, the main commercial gallery area of New York. Suzanne had her first one-woman exhibit there in early 1975. In that same year she assumed another responsibility on the west coast. Governor Brown of California appointed her to the California Arts Commission, a group of people from all the arts that sets policy for the arts in the state.

Ankrum Gallery continued to hold one-woman exhibits for Suzanne. At her second solo exhibit, Suzanne was pleased to see that her new, very large paintings filled the entire gallery. She explains that in painting the large canvases in her new loose style she might cover the canvas with a hundred to a hundred and fifty layers of acrylic paint and washes. Sometimes images are applied in bright colors and then pale washes are painted over them so they appear as only a shadow when the painting is completed. She points to *Eclypse,* which started out as a bright blue primed canvas. The images, two figures floating over a heart, are painted in a delicate play of all of the layers of paint. Curved lines give the painting a feeling of graceful movement.

Another painting, *Animal,* seems to have no other animal than a bird along with its colored shapes. Finally,

Suzanne Jackson, Animal, *1974.*

the viewer can make out the delicate image of a puppy, washed over with many layers of white paint. *Animal* was purchased for the newest major art museum in the United States. Joseph Hirshorn donated his extensive collection of American art to the Smithsonian Institution with the stipulation that the government build a museum to house the collection. In the autumn of 1974 the Hirshorn Museum opened in Washington, D.C. A round, contemporary building, it shelters the finest examples of contemporary American art. Suzanne Jackson's painting will join this distinguished company.

Even while her works hung at Ankrum, Suzanne was most excited about the new ideas she was using in the paintings in her studio. She was fascinated with contrasting tones of white and with the relationship of underpainted bright colors to the surface layers of washes and white paint. Then, gradually, she explored the idea of relating the figures in the paintings more to the background. The background changed subtly from the pale white to warmer tones of silver and gold with the white or creamy tones. Her personal life shifted too, when she married Wayne Leonard in early 1975. Both of them lead creative lives. Wayne is advertising director for the *Los Angeles Free Press*. And Suzanne feels more relaxed and free to explore the new ideas in her art work since her marriage. "I feel like I'm just beginning to paint," she says.

Considering the success she has achieved in a short time, Suzanne Jackson seems to be at the beginning of a career that will bring her many honors and a reputation that will place her among the major artists of our time. How interesting it will be to follow her work when it is exhibited in California, New York, and at places in between!

Other Outstanding Women

In addition to the six women featured in this book, there are many hundreds more who have contributed greatly to the world of art. Although it is impossible to discuss them all, here are a few more of the foremost women in art.

LILLY MARTIN SPENCER (1811-1902). Lilly Martin Spencer earned enough money from her paintings to comfortably support a family of seven children. While she spent her day painting, often using her own children for models, her husband cared for the house and children. One of the most popular American artists of the mid-1800s, she had almost no formal art training. She had taken only a few classes when she was ten years old, and later, as a young woman, she received criticism and advice from professional artists in Cincinnati. But she quickly mastered techniques of painting and in 1848, after successful exhibits of her work in New York, decided to move to that city. Today the domestic scenes that Spencer painted are considered sentimental and overly romantic. But in her time they reflected public taste. More than a million copies of her paintings were published as lithographs and engravings, which people hung in their homes. Her illustrations appeared in *Godey's Ladies Book,* a popular magazine of that period. She also painted many portraits for commissions, and they are considered her best art work.

PEGGY GUGGENHEIM (1898-   ). Not an artist herself, but an avid collector of modern art, Peggy Guggenheim's contribution is as important to us as the creation of paintings and sculptures themselves. She has donated hundreds of paintings to museums, sent exhibits of her collection throughout the world, and opened her home in Venice to the public. Peggy inherited a fortune at age nineteen, and a fortune is one requirement for buying good quality, original art works. But Peggy also possessed others—innate good taste and courage to select paintings of unknown artists. In her Art of This Century Gallery in New York, Guggenheim gave the first one-man shows for Jackson Pollock, Robert Motherwell, and other innovators of abstract expressionism. Before Pollock was able to sell his work, she offered him a contract that gave him a monthly salary. The Art of This Century Gallery lasted only from 1942 to 1947, but its influence on modern art is permanent.

ALICE NEEL (1900-   ). Calling herself a "collector of souls," Alice Neel paints the human figure. Her portraits probe personality traits; they give clues to the way the subject lived his or her life—timidly or brashly. Neel is not afraid to paint sagging flesh and deep lines; ravages of age and time. Since taking her art training at the Philadelphia School of Design for Women, Neel has steadfastly painted human subjects through each new wave of American art: modernism, cubism, abstract expressionism, and all of the post-abstract movements. In the 1970s she has received honors and recognition for skills she long possessed. A retrospective exhibition of her work was held at the Whitney Museum, and people flocked to the opening.

LEE KRASNER (about 1914-   ). A first-generation abstract expressionist painter, Lee Krasner exhibited in the first group showings of this new style of painting in New York in the early 1940s. Her art training started the traditional way, copying antique statues at the Women's Art School of Cooper Union. Later, at the National Academy of Design, she painted a self-portrait of unusual strength that has been reproduced many times. Lee claims that she painted it to "get promoted from drawing to life." Working in a second floor studio in the Long Island home she shared with her husband, Jackson Pollock, Lee painted a series of black and white abstract paintings with forms that looked like mysterious letters or hieroglyphics. About 1950 she altered her style and began to use thinner paints. Later dissatisfied with these works, she cut them into pieces and combined them with other scraps to create collages, paintings made of pasted shapes of contrasting materials. Critics wrote that the new combinations were more powerful than the older works. Lee and her husband would never enter each other's studios unless invited to view work in progress—this was evidence of the respect they accorded each other as artists. Lee Krasner's work hangs in the Philadelphia and Whitney Museums and in numerous private collections.

GRACE HARTIGAN (1922-   ). Grace Hartigan's training consisted of private classes with Isaac Lane Muse and also the stimulating company of young artists interested in abstract expressionism in New York in the late 1940s and 1950s. She was among the young artists who gathered at the Artist's Club to argue about the theories of the new art. She also exhibited at Tibor de

Nagy Gallery. About 1960 Hartigan's yearly exhibits began to appear at the Martha Jackson Gallery. Although she belongs to the New York School of painters, Hartigan practices her own version of abstract expressionism. In some of her works, the colors swirl on the surface of the canvas in entirely abstract images; at other times she paints recognizable images, human shapes, street scenes, or still lifes. At the present time Grace Hartigan's bold, complicated paintings hang in the permanent collections of virtually every important museum in the United States. Vivid thick pigments, deep green and blue opposing hot pink and orange, suggest a painter in love with paint and color.

JOAN MITCHELL (1926-   ). Joan Mitchell paints landscapes—not scenes of a pretty meadow below a cloud-studded sky—but landscapes literally of paint. Great patches of blue drip over squares of white; other patches of brown and gold simply suggest a thick tangle of weeds. The patches of color seem to float over a ground of open or white canvas that suggests the bright light of a sunny day, perhaps in the French countryside, where Joan Mitchell has chosen to live for the past several years. Even the size of her paintings suggests a vast open field—her canvases are sometimes twenty feet long. Educated at Smith College, Columbia University, the Art Institute of Chicago, and New York University, Mitchell had intense art training that was the best that can be had in art schools. A 1974 retrospective exhibit at the Whitney Museum received enthusiastic reviews for the great beauty and freshness of her paintings. Mitchell's works may be viewed in museums in Europe and throughout the United States.

MARISOL ESCOBAR (1930-   ). Marisol, as she is known to everyone, is a pop artist. Artists of this movement of the early 1960s took images familiar to everyone, blew them up to incredible size, and then painted or sculpted them true to life. Pop art is humorous; it is as though the artists said of the objects, "Look at me; really look at me." Marisol took for her subjects popular figures like President Lyndon Johnson, painted them on sheets of plyboard, and then cut around them and exhibited them like the flat figures of a stage set. Her later work focuses on prints, but Marisol still chooses familiar images. Faces, feet, and hands, especially her own, seem to be her favorites. Although she was born in Paris and educated at Ecole des Beaux Arts, she lives in the United States and works in an art movement as American as the Campbell's soup cans it often pictures. Her work is represented in important museums and reproduced in textbooks on contemporary art.

ELEANOR CREEKMORE DICKINSON (1931-   ). Creating whole environments, not simply one painting or sculpture, is the specialty of Eleanor Dickinson. Her most successful work, called *Revival,* recreated a religious tent meeting, complete with wooden folding chairs, hymnals, paper fans, and pulpit. When *Revival* was exhibited, taped revival hymns played continuously in the background. Her incredibly strong line-drawings of people who attended revival meetings lined the walls. When the work was exhibited in Tennessee, a preacher standing in the environment was so moved that he stepped into the pulpit and began to deliver a sermon. Dickinson's birth in the hills of eastern Tennessee and education in Knoxville perhaps gave her the sensitivity to have picked out the right details to construct *Revival.* This work was exhibited in several museums, including the Corcoran Gallery of Art in Washington, D.C. Although she now makes her home in San Francisco, Dickinson returns many summers to Appalachia to listen to the dialect and to record the songs and ballads of the mountains. In her hand is the paper and black felt-tipped pen that she uses to make her compelling drawings of the people as they shout, cry, and pray.

JUDY CHICAGO (1939-   ). After a long, conscious struggle, the artist Judy Chicago discovered the woman Judy Chicago. She believes that this self-knowledge is essential to freeing the creative abilities of any woman who is an artist. In her classes at the Feminist Studio Workshop at the Women's Building in Los Angeles, she teaches her students to first become conscious of their feelings and desires as women. Then they learn the traditional art skills—perspective, modeling, and color theory—that give them techniques to express their feelings. Along with art skills, the women learn carpentry, so that they can create their own studio space, install art, and make their own stretchers. Judy Chicago's own art is an example of what she teaches. Beautiful posters and paintings, with abstract images sprayed in acrylic paints, symbolize womanliness—rounded gentle shapes and strong aggressive images. Publication of her autobiography, *Through the Flower, My Struggle as a Woman Artist,* in 1975, occurred during a busy year: she taught, created many artistic works, undertook administrative duties and speaking engagements, and spent time in her home with her husband. Any one of these activities might have filled the time of someone less energetic and less committed to her art than Judy Chicago.

Suggested Reading

Breeskin, Adelyn D. *Mary Cassatt*. Smithsonian Institution Press, 1970.
A catalogue of all of Mary Cassatt's paintings with accurate records of their ownership.

Chicago, Judy. *Through the Flower: My Struggle as a Woman Artist*. Doubleday, 1975.
An autobiography that presents the artist's life and career from a feminist viewpoint.

Friedman, Martin. *Nevelson Wood Sculptures*. Dutton, 1973.
The catalogue for Louise Nevelson's latest retrospective exhibit with an interesting essay interpreting her assemblage technique.

Glimcher, Arnold B. *Louise Nevelson*. Praeger, 1972.
Written by her current dealer, this large art book contains dramatic photographs of Nevelson's sculptures and a biography of the artist.

Goodrich, Lloyd and Bry, Doris. *Georgia O'Keeffe*. Whitney Museum of American Art, 1970.
A brief biography of the artist introduces photographs of her paintings, including many in color.

Goossen, E. C. *Helen Frankenthaler*. Praeger, 1969.
A discussion of the artist's soak-stain method and her place in art history, written by one of her friends.

Kallir, Otto. *Grandma Moses*. Abrams, 1973.
An art book with reproductions of all of Grandma Moses' paintings, many full-page size and in color. The book includes an interesting biography.

Lewis, Samnella and Waddy, Ruth. *Black Artists on Art*. Vol. 2. Ward, Richie Press, 1971.
A collection of photographed art works of several black artists, including Suzanne Jackson, with comments by the artists on their work.

Moore, Clement. *The Night before Christmas*. Illustrated by Grandma Moses. Random House, 1961.
Grandma Moses' illustrations for this classic Christmas story delight any age.

Moses, Anna Mary Robertson. *Grandma Moses: American Primitive*. Edited by Otto Kallir. Dryden Press, 1946.
Photographs of Grandma Moses' paintings with her lively remarks about them.

Rose, Barbara. *Frankenthaler*. Abrams, 1970.
A large art book with beautiful colored reproductions of Helen Frankenthaler's paintings, a brief biography of her working life, and insights into her technique.

Sweet, Frederick A. *Miss Mary Cassatt: Impressionist from Pennsylvania*. University of Oklahoma, 1966.
An interesting, readable biography of Mary Cassatt that includes excerpts from letters written by the artist.

Wilder, Mitchell. *Georgia O'Keeffe: An Exhibition of the Work of the Artist from 1915 to 1966*. Amon Carter Museum of Western Art, 1966.
Brief written commentary on the art works includes several penetrating remarks by the artist herself in this catalogue.

Wilson, Ellen. *An American Painter in Paris, The Life of Mary Cassatt*. Farrar, Straus and Giroux, 1971.
This lively biography, written for young readers, traces the career of Mary Cassatt from discouragement to triumph.

Carol Fowler is a free-lance writer who has contributed both short stories and nonfiction articles to a number of young people's magazines, including *Ingenue, Twelve-Fifteen,* and *Teen Time.*

Ms. Fowler received her B.S. degree from the University of Wisconsin at Madison. After graduation, she taught science at the eighth-grade level for several years. She is currently a member of the California Writer's Club and the American Association of University Women.

She and her husband have three children and live in Walnut Grove, California. Ms. Fowler is also a volunteer tour guide at the Walnut Creek Civic Arts Gallery, where she conducts groups of school children through contemporary art exhibits.